The Meaning of Life: A Very Short Introduction

'warm intellectual pleasure ... meticulous treatment of the subject. ... It looks like Eagleton got it right.'

Mario Pisani, *The Financial Times*

'A charming personal voyage round himself, I can only say it left me thoroughly surprised – and delighted.'
Simon Jenkins, *Times Literary Supplement* Books of the Year

'The name Terry Eagleton ... assures us of stimulation, style, sparkling, sometimes acerbic, wit, and wide-ranging erudition. In other words he is eminently readable ... [a] commendably pocket-sized book.'

Gordon Parsons, *Morning Star*

'The book's a little gem'
Suzanne Harrington, *Irish Examiner*

'It is a stimulating and often entertaining ... Cook's tour around the chief monuments of western philosophy and literature ... *The Meaning of Life* is unusual and refreshing.'

John Gray, *The Independent*

'A lively starting point for late-night debate'
John Cornwell, *The Sunday Times*

VERY SHORT INTRODUCTIONS are for anyone wanting a stimulating and accessible way into a new subject. They are written by experts, and have been translated into more than 45 different languages.

The series began in 1995, and now covers a wide variety of topics in every discipline. The VSI library now contains over 500 volumes—a Very Short Introduction to everything from Psychology and Philosophy of Science to American History and Relativity—and continues to grow in every subject area.

Titles in the series include the following:

Terry Eagleton

THE MEANING
OF LIFE

A Very Short Introduction

OXFORD
UNIVERSITY PRESS

OXFORD

UNIVERSITY PRESS

Great Clarendon Street, Oxford OX2 6DP

Oxford University Press is a department of the University of Oxford.
It furthers the University's objective of excellence in research, scholarship,
and education by publishing worldwide in

Oxford New York

Auckland Cape Town Dar es Salaam Hong Kong Karachi
Kuala Lumpur Madrid Melbourne Mexico City Nairobi
New Delhi Shanghai Taipei Toronto

With offices in

Argentina Austria Brazil Chile Czech Republic France Greece
Guatemala Hungary Italy Japan Poland Portugal Singapore
South Korea Switzerland Thailand Turkey Ukraine Vietnam

Published in the United States
by Oxford University Press Inc., New York

First published in hardback 2007

First published as a Very Short Introduction 2008

British Library Cataloguing in Publication Data

Data available

Library of Congress Cataloging in Publication Data

Eagleton, Terry, 1943–
The meaning of life: a very short introduction / Terry Eagleton.
p. cm.
Includes index.
ISBN-13: 978-0-19-953217-9
1. Life. 2. Meaning (Philosophy) I. Title.
BD431.E14   2008
128–dc22   2007051203

ISBN 978-0-19-953217-9

Typeset by SPI Publisher Services, Pondicherry, India

Printed and bound by
CPI Group (UK) Ltd, Croydon, CR0 4YY

For Oliver, who found the whole idea deeply embarrassing

Contents

List of illustrations

The publisher and the author apologize for any errors or omissions in the above list. If contacted they will be pleased to rectify these at the earliest opportunity.

Preface

Anyone rash enough to write a book with a title like this had better brace themselves for a postbag crammed with letters in erratic handwriting enclosing complex symbolic diagrams. The meaning of life is a subject fit for either the crazed or the comic, and I hope I have fallen more into the latter camp than the former. I have tried to treat a high-minded topic as lightly and lucidly as possible, while at the same time taking it seriously. But there is something absurdly overreaching about the whole subject, in contrast to the more miniature scale of academic scholarship. Years ago, when I was a student in Cambridge, my eye was caught by the title of a doctoral thesis which read 'Some aspects of the vaginal system of the flea'. It was not, one would guess, the most suitable work for those with poor eyesight; but it revealed an appealing modesty that I have apparently failed to learn from. I can at least claim to have written one of the very few meaning-of-life books which does not recount the story of Bertrand Russell and the taxi driver.

I am very grateful to Joseph Dunne, who read the book in manuscript and made some invaluable criticisms and suggestions.

TE

Chapters 1
Questions and answers

Philosophers have an infuriating habit of analysing questions rather than answering them, and this is how I want to begin.[1] Is 'What is the meaning of life?' a genuine question, or does it just look like one? Is there anything that could count as an answer to it, or is it really a kind of pseudo-question, like the legendary Oxford examination question which is supposed to have read simply: 'Is this a good question?'

'What is the meaning of life?' looks at first glance like the same kind of question as 'What is the capital of Albania?', or 'What is the colour of ivory?' But is it really? Could it be more like 'What is the taste of geometry?'

There is one fairly standard reason why some thinkers regard the meaning-of-life question as being itself meaningless. This is the case that meaning is a matter of language, not objects. It is a question of the way we talk about things, not a feature of things themselves, like texture, weight, or colour. A cabbage or a cardiograph is not meaningful in itself; it becomes so only by being caught up in our conversations. On this theory, we can make life meaningful by our talk about it; but it cannot have a meaning

---

[1] Perhaps I should add that I am not myself a philosopher, a fact which I am sure some of my reviewers will point out in any case.

in itself, any more than a cloud can. It would not make sense, for example, to speak of a cloud as being either true or false. Rather, truth and falsehood are functions of our human propositions about clouds. There are problems with this argument, as there are with most philosophical arguments. We shall be looking at a few of them later on.

Let us take a brief look at an even more imposing query than 'What is the meaning of life?' Perhaps the most fundamental question it is possible to raise is 'Why is there anything at all, rather than nothing?' Why is there anything about which we can ask 'What does it mean?' in the first place? Philosophers are divided about whether this is a real question or a bogus one, though theologians for the most part are not. For most theologians, the answer to this inquiry is 'God'. God is said to be 'Creator' of the universe not because he is some kind of mega-manufacturer, but because he is the reason why there is something rather than nothing. He is, as they say, the ground of being. And this would still be true of him even if the universe had no beginning. He would still be the reason why there is something rather than nothing even if there has been something from all eternity.

'Why is there anything and not just nothing?' could be roughly translated as 'How come the cosmos?' This could be taken as a question about causality – in which case, 'How come?' would mean 'Where does it come from?' But this is surely not what the query means. If we tried to answer the question by talking about how the universe got off the ground in the first place, then those causes must themselves be part of everything, and we are back to where we started. Only a cause which was not part of everything – one which transcended the universe, as God is supposed to do – could avoid being dragged back into the argument in this way. So this is not really a question about how the world came about. Nor, for theologians at least, is it a question about what the world is *for*, since in their opinion the world has no purpose whatsoever. God is not a celestial engineer who created the world with some strategically calculated goal in mind. He is an artist who created it simply for his own self-delight, and for the self-delight of Creation itself. It is understandable, then, why he is widely considered to have something of a twisted sense of humour.

'Why is there anything rather than nothing?' is rather an expression of wonderment that there is a world in the first place, when there could presumably quite easily have been nothing. Perhaps this is part of what Ludwig Wittgenstein has in mind when he remarks that 'Not how the world is, is the mystical, but *that* it is'.[2] This, one might claim, is Wittgenstein's version of what the German philosopher Martin Heidegger calls the *Seinsfrage*, or question of Being. 'How come Being?' is the question to which Heidegger wants to return. He is less interested in how particular entities came about, than in the mind-bending fact that there are entities in the first place. And these things are open to our understanding, as they might easily not have been.

For many philosophers, however, not least Anglo-Saxon ones, 'How come Being?' is a supreme example of a pseudo-question. In their view, it would not only be difficult, if not impossible, to know how to answer it; it is deeply doubtful that there is anything there to be answered. For them, it is really just a ponderous Teutonic way of saying 'Wow!' It may be a valid question for the poet or mystic, but not for the philosopher. And in the Anglo-Saxon world in particular, the barricades between the two camps are vigilantly manned.

In a work like *Philosophical Investigations*, Wittgenstein was alert to the difference between real questions and phoney ones. A piece of language can have the grammatical form of a question but not actually be one. Or our grammar can mislead

[2] Ludwig Wittgenstein, *Tractatus Logico-Philosophicus* (London, 1961), 6.44.

us into mistaking one kind of proposition for another. 'What then, fellow countrymen, once the enemy is vanquished, can we not accomplish in the hour of victory?' sounds like a question anticipating an answer, but is in fact a rhetorical question, to which one would probably be ill-advised to return the reply: 'Nothing'. The utterance is cast in interrogative form simply to enhance its dramatic force. 'So what?', 'Why don't you get lost?', and 'What are you staring at?' sound like questions but aren't really. 'Whereabouts in the body is the soul?' might sound like a reasonable sort of question to pose, but only because we are thinking along the lines of a question like 'Whereabouts in the body are the kidneys?' 'Where is my envy?' has the form of a kosher question, but only because we are unconsciously modelling it on 'Where is my armpit?'

Wittgenstein came to believe that a great many philosophical puzzles arise out of people misusing language in this way. Take, for example, the statement 'I have a pain', which is grammatically akin to 'I have a hat'. This similarity might mislead us into thinking that pains, or 'experiences' in general, are things we have in the same way that we have hats. But it would be strange to say 'Here, take my pain'. And though it would make sense to say 'Is this your hat or mine?', it would sound odd to ask 'Is this your pain or mine?' Perhaps there are several people in a room and a pain floating around in it; and as each person in turn doubles up in agony, we exclaim: 'Ah, now *he's* having it!'

This sounds merely silly; but in fact it has some fairly momentous implications. Wittgenstein is able to disentangle the grammar of 'I have a hat' from 'I have a pain' not only in a way that throws light on the use of personal pronouns like 'I' and 'he', but in ways which undermine the long-standing assumption that my experiences are a kind of private property. In fact, they seem even more like private property than my hat, since I can give away my hat, but not my pain. Wittgenstein shows us how grammar deceives us

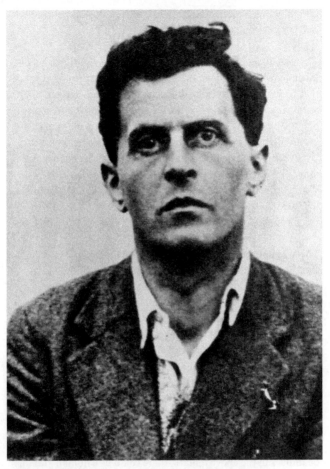

1. Ludwig Wittgenstein, commonly thought to be the greatest philosopher of the twentieth century

into thinking this way, and his case has radical, even politically radical, consequences.

The task of the philosopher, Wittgenstein thought, was not so much to resolve these inquiries as to *dissolve* them – to show that they spring from confusing one kind of 'language game', as he called it, with another. We are bewitched by the structure of our language, and the philosopher's job was to demystify us, disentangling different uses of words. Language, because it inevitably has a degree of uniformity about it, tends to make different kinds of utterance look pretty much the same. So Wittgenstein toyed with the idea of appending as an epigraph to his *Philosophical Investigations* a quotation from *King Lear*: 'I'll teach you differences'.

This was not a view confined to Wittgenstein alone. One of the greatest of all nineteenth-century philosophers, Friedrich Nietzsche, anticipated it when he wondered whether it was because of our grammar that we had failed to get rid of God. Since our grammar allows us to construct nouns, which represent distinct entities, then it also makes it seem plausible that there can be a kind of Noun of nouns, a mega-entity known as God, without which all the little entities around us might simply collapse. Nietzsche, however, believed neither in mega-entities nor in everyday ones. He thought the very idea of there being distinct objects, such as God or gooseberries, was just a reifying effect of language. He certainly believed this about the individual self, which he saw as no more than a convenient fiction. Perhaps, so he implies in the above remark, there could be a human grammar in which this reifying operation was not possible. Perhaps this will be the language of the future, one spoken by the *Übermensch* or Meta-man who has got beyond nouns and discrete entities altogether, and therefore beyond God and similar metaphysical illusions. The philosopher Jacques Derrida, a thinker much indebted to Nietzsche, is rather more pessimistic in this respect. For him, as for Wittgenstein, such metaphysical illusions are built into the very structure of our language, and cannot be eradicated. The philosopher must simply wage a ceaseless, Canute-like war against them – a battle which Wittgenstein sees as a kind of linguistic therapy, and which Derrida terms 'deconstruction'.[3]

Just as Nietzsche thought that nouns were reifying, so someone might think this of the word 'life' in the question 'What is the meaning of life?' We shall be looking at this more closely later. It might also be thought that the question models itself unconsciously on a different kind of question altogether, and that this is where it goes wrong. We can say 'This is worth a dollar, and so is that, so how much are they worth altogether?'; so it feels as though we can also say 'This bit of life has meaning, and so has that bit, so what meaning do all the various bits add up to?' But it does not follow from the fact that the parts have meaning that the whole has a meaning over and above them, any more than it follows that a lot of little things add up to one big thing simply because they are all coloured pink.

All this, to be sure, brings us no nearer to the meaning of life. Yet questions are worth examining, since the nature of a question is important in determining what might count as an answer to it. In fact, it could be claimed that it is questions, not answers, which are the difficult thing. It is well known what kind of answer a silly question provokes. Posing the right kind of question can open up a whole new continent of knowledge, bringing other vital queries tumbling in its wake. Some philosophers, of a so-called hermeneutical turn of mind, see reality as whatever it is that returns an answer to a question. And reality, which like a veteran criminal does not just spontaneously pipe up without first being interrogated, will only respond to us in accordance with the kinds of inquiries we put to it. Karl Marx once observed somewhat cryptically that human beings only pose such problems as they

---

[3] For a more detailed discussion, see my 'Wittgenstein's Friends', in *Against the Grain* (London, 1986).

can resolve – meaning perhaps that if we have the conceptual apparatus to pose the question, then we already have in principle the means to determine an answer to it.

This is partly because questions are not posed in a vacuum. It is true that they do not have their answers tied conveniently to their tails; but they intimate the kind of response that would at least count as an answer. They point us in a limited range of directions, suggesting where to look for a solution. It would not be hard to write the history of knowledge in terms of the kind of questions men and women have thought it possible or necessary to raise. Not any question is possible at any given time. Rembrandt could not ask whether photography had rendered realist painting redundant.

This is not of course to suggest that all questions are answerable. We tend to assume that where there is a problem there must be a solution, just as we tend rather oddly to imagine that things which are in fragments should always be put back together again. But there are plenty of problems to which we will probably never discover solutions, along with questions which will go eternally unanswered. There is no record of how many hairs adorned Napoleon's head when he died, and now we shall never know. Perhaps the human brain is simply not up to resolving certain questions, such as the origins of intelligence. Perhaps this is because there is no evolutionary need for us to do so, though there is no evolutionary need for us to understand *Finnegans Wake* or the laws of physics either. There are also questions to which we do not know the answers because there are in fact no answers, such as how many children Lady Macbeth had, or whether Sherlock Holmes had a small mole on his inner thigh. We cannot answer this last question in the negative any more than we can reply to it in the affirmative.

It is possible, then, that there is indeed an answer to the meaning-of-life question, but that we shall never know what it is. If this is so, then we are in something like the situation of the narrator of Henry James's story 'The Figure in the Carpet', who is told by a celebrated author he admires that there is a concealed design in his work, one implicit in every image and turn of phrase. But the author dies before the baffled, frantically curious narrator can discover what it is. Perhaps the author was having him on. Or maybe he thought there was such a design in his work, but there wasn't. Or perhaps the narrator is somehow seeing the design all along without grasping the fact that he has grasped it. Or maybe any design he himself manages to construct will do.

It is even conceivable that not knowing the meaning of life is part of the meaning of life, rather as not counting how many words I am uttering when I give an after-dinner speech helps me to give an after-dinner speech. Perhaps life is kept going by our ignorance of its fundamental meaning, as capitalism is for Karl Marx. The philosopher Arthur Schopenhauer thought something of the kind, and so in a sense did Sigmund Freud. For the Nietzsche of *The Birth of Tragedy*, the true meaning of life is too terrible for us to cope with, which is why we need our consoling illusions if we are to carry on. What we call 'life' is just a necessary fiction. Without a huge admixture of fantasy, reality would grind to a halt.

There are moral problems, too, to which no solution can be had. Because there are different kinds of moral goods, such as courage, compassion, justice, and so on, and because these values are sometimes incommensurable with one another, it is possible for them to enter into tragic conflict with each other. As the sociologist Max Weber bleakly remarked: 'The ultimately possible attitudes to life are irreconcilable, and hence their struggle can never be brought to a final conclusion.'[4] Isaiah Berlin writes in similar vein that 'the world that we encounter in ordinary

[4] Max Weber, *Essays in Sociology*, ed. H. H. Gerth and C. Wright Mills (London, 1991), 152.

experience is one in which we are faced by choices equally absolute, the realisation of some of which must inevitably mean the sacrifice of others'.[5] This, one might say, reflects a certain tragic vein of liberalism, which, unlike the callow cult of 'choice' or 'options' of our own day, is prepared to reckon the devastating cost of its commitment to liberty and diversity. It also contrasts with a more up-beat brand of liberalism for which plurality is inherently beneficial and the conflict between moral values invariably energizing. But the truth is that there just are situations from which one can emerge only with dirty hands. Pressed far enough, every moral law starts to come apart at the seams. The novelist Thomas Hardy was well aware that you can paint yourself unwittingly into moral corners in which, whichever way you move, someone is bound to get badly damaged. There is simply no answer to the question of which of your children you should sacrifice if a Nazi soldier orders you to hand over one of them to be killed.[6]

Something of the same goes for political life as well. It is surely clear that the only ultimate solution to terrorism is political justice. Terrorism, however atrocious, is not in this sense irrational: there are situations such as Northern Ireland in which those who use terror to promote their political ends come to recognize that their demands for justice and equality are at last being partly met, conclude that the use of terror has now become counterproductive, and agree to abandon it. As far as Islamic fundamentalist terror goes, however, there are those who claim that even if Arab demands were to be fulfilled – if a just solution to the Palestine/Israeli question were to be implemented, US military bases banished from Arab territory, and so on – the slaying and maiming of innocent civilians would carry on.

[5] Isaiah Berlin, *Four Essays on Liberty* (Oxford, 1969), 168.
[6] For a useful discussion of moral dilemmas, see Rosalind Hursthouse, *On Virtue Ethics* (Oxford, 1999), ch. 3.

Perhaps it would. But this may be to say no more than that the problem has now escalated beyond all feasible resolution. This need not be a defeatist judgement, simply realistic. Destructive forces which spring from remediable causes can take on a lethal momentum of their own which there is finally no stopping. Perhaps it is now simply too late to staunch the spreading of terrorism. In which case there is no solution to the problem of terrorism – a proposition that would be impossible for most politicians to voice publicly, and one that is profoundly unpalatable to most other people, not least chronically up-beat Americans. Even so, it may be the truth. Why should one imagine that when there is a problem there is always a solution?

One of most powerful meaning-of-life questions without an up-beat solution is known as tragedy. Of all artistic forms, tragedy is the one that confronts the meaning-of-life question most searchingly and unswervingly, intrepidly prepared as it is to entertain the most horrific of responses to it. Tragedy at its finest is a courageous reflection on the fundamental nature of human existence, and has its origin in an ancient Greek culture in which life is fragile, perilous, and sickeningly vulnerable. For the ancient tragedians, the world is only fitfully penetrable by the frail light of reason; past deeds weigh in upon present aspirations to strangle them at birth; and men and women find themselves languishing in the grip of brutally vindictive forces which threaten to tear them to pieces. Only by keeping your head down as you pick a precarious way through the minefield of human existence can you hope to survive, paying homage to cruelly capricious gods who often enough scarcely deserve human respect, let alone religious veneration. The very human powers which might allow you to find a foothold in this unstable terrain continually threaten to spin out of control, turning against you and bringing you low. It is in these fearful conditions that the Chorus of Sophocles' *Oedipus the King* delivers its final gloomy judgement: 'Count no man happy till he dies, free of pain at last.'

This may be a response to the problem of human existence, but it is hardly a solution to it. For tragedy, there is often enough no answer to why individual lives are crushed and mutilated beyond endurance, why injustice and oppression appear to reign sovereign in human affairs, or why men are deceived into chewing the roasted flesh of their own slaughtered children. Or rather, the only answer lies in the resilience with which these issues are confronted, the depth and artistry with which they are framed. Tragedy at its most potent is a question without an answer, deliberately depriving us of ideological consolation. If it demonstrates in its every gesture that human existence cannot tolerably carry on like this, it challenges us to find a solution to its anguish which is more than just another piece of wishful thinking, piecemeal reformism, sentimental humanism, or idealist panacea. In portraying a world in urgent need of redemption, it intimates at the same moment that the very thought of redemption may well be just another way of distracting ourselves from a terror which threatens to turn us to stone.[7]

Heidegger argues in his work *Being and Time* that humans are distinguished from other beings by their capacity to put their own existence into question. They are the creatures for whom existence as such, not just particular features of it, is problematic. This or that situation might prove problematic for a warthog, but – so the theory goes – humans are those peculiar animals who confront their own situation as a question, quandary, source of anxiety, ground of hope, burden, gift, dread, or absurdity. And this is not least because they are aware, as warthogs presumably are not, that their existence is finite. Human beings are perhaps the only animals who live in the perpetual shadow of death.

All the same, there is something distinctively 'modern' about Heidegger's case. It is not, of course, that Aristotle or Attila the

---

[7] I have written more fully on the idea of tragedy in *Sweet Violence: The Idea of the Tragic* (Oxford, 2003).

Hun were not conscious of being mortal, though the latter was probably more conscious of other people's mortality than his own. It is also true that human beings, not least because they have language, are capable of objectifying their own existence in a way that tortoises presumably are not. We can speak of something called the 'human condition', whereas it is unlikely that tortoises brood under the shelter of their shells on the condition of being a tortoise. Tortoises are in this sense remarkably similar to postmodernists, to whom the idea of the human condition is equally alien. Language, in other words, allows us not only to get a fix on ourselves, but to conceive of our situation as a whole. Because we live by signs, which bring along with them the capacity for abstraction, we can distance ourselves from our immediate contexts, free ourselves from the imprisonment of our bodily senses, and speculate on the human situation as such. Like fire, however, the power of abstraction is an ambiguous gift, at once creative and destructive. If it allows us to think in terms of whole communities, it also allows us to lay them waste with chemical weapons.

Distancing of this kind does not involve leaping out of our skins, or gazing down on the world from some Olympian vantage-point. To meditate on our being in the world is part of our way of being in the world. Even if 'the human situation as such' turns out to be a metaphysical mirage, as postmodern thought insists, it remains a conceivable object of speculation. So there is something, no doubt, to Heidegger's claim. Other animals may be anxious about, say, escaping predators or feeding their young, but they do not give the appearance of being troubled by what has been called 'ontological anxiety': namely, the feeling (sometimes accompanied by a particularly intense hangover) that one is a pointless, superfluous being – a 'useless passion', as Jean-Paul Sartre put it.

Even so, talk of dread, anxiety, nausea, absurdity, and the like as characteristic of the human condition is a lot more common among twentieth-century artists and philosophers than it is among twelfth-century ones. What marks modernist thought from one end to another is the belief that human existence is *contingent* – that it has no ground, goal, direction, or necessity, and that our species might quite easily never have emerged on the planet. This possibility then hollows out our actual presence, casting across it the perpetual shadow of loss and death. Even in our most ecstatic moments, we are dimly aware that the ground is marshy underfoot – that there is no unimpeachable foundation to what we are and what we do. This may make our finest moments even more precious, or it may serve to drastically devalue them.

This is not a viewpoint which would have rallied much support among twelfth-century philosophers, for whom there was a solid foundation to human existence known as God. Yet even for them, this did not mean that our presence in the world was necessary. Indeed, it would have been heretical to think so. To claim that God transcends his own Creation is to say among other things that he did not need to bring it about. He did so out of love, not need. And that includes bringing us about as well. Human existence is gratuitous – a matter of grace and gift – rather than indispensable. God could have got on perfectly well without us, and would have had a much quieter life had he done so. Like the father of some appalling little brat, he might well have lived to regret his decision to go in for paternity. Human beings first of all disobeyed his laws, and then, to add insult to injury, lost faith in him altogether while continuing to flout his commands.

There may be a sense, then, in which inquiring after the meaning of life is a permanent possibility for human beings – part, indeed, of what makes us the kind of creatures we are. Job in the Old Testament raises the question quite as insistently as Jean-Paul Sartre. Yet for most ancient Hebrews, the question was presumably irrelevant because the answer was obvious. Yahweh and his Law were the meaning of life, and not to recognize this would have been well-nigh unthinkable. Even Job, for whom human existence (or at least his own bit of it) is all a dreadful mistake which ought to be called off as soon as possible, acknowledges Yahweh's omnipotent presence.

The question 'What is the meaning of life? might have seemed to an ancient Hebrew as curious as the question 'Do you believe in God?' For most people today, including a lot of religious believers, the latter question is unconsciously modelled on questions like 'Do you believe in Father Christmas?', or 'Do you believe in alien abductions?' On this view, there are certain beings, all the way from God and the Yeti to the Loch Ness monster and the crew of UFOs, who may or may not exist. The evidence is equivocal, and opinion is accordingly divided on the matter. But an ancient Hebrew would probably not have imagined that 'Do you believe in God?' meant anything like that. Since the presence of Yahweh was proclaimed by the whole earth and heavens, the question could only mean: 'Do you have faith in him?' It was a matter of a practice, not of an intellectual proposition. It asked about a relationship, not about an opinion.

Perhaps, then, pre-modern peoples in general, despite Heidegger's very general claims, were less plagued by the meaning-of-life question than we moderns are. This was not only because their religious beliefs were less up for question, but because their social practices were less problematic as well. Perhaps the meaning of life in such conditions consists in doing more or less what your ancestors did, and what age-old social conventions expect of you. Religion and mythology are there to instruct you in what basically matters. The idea that there could be a meaning to your life which was peculiar to you, quite different from the meaning of other people's lives, would not have mustered many votes. By and large, the meaning of your life consisted of its function within a greater whole. Outside this context, you were simply an empty signifier. The word 'individual' originally means 'indivisible' or 'inseparable from'. Homer's Odysseus seems to feel roughly this way, whereas Shakespeare's Hamlet most definitely does not.

Feeling that the meaning of your life is a function of a greater whole is not at all incompatible with having a robust sense of selfhood. It is the meaning of individual selfhood, not the reality of it, which is at stake here. This is not to say that pre-modern people did not ask themselves who they were or what they were doing here. It is simply that they seem for the most part to have been less agitated by the question than, say, Albert Camus or the early T. S. Eliot. And this has much to do with their religious faith.

If pre-modern cultures were generally less bothered by the meaning of life than Franz Kafka, the same would seem to be true of postmodern ones. In the pragmatist, streetwise climate of advanced postmodern capitalism, with its scepticism of big pictures and grand narratives, its hard-nosed disenchantment with the metaphysical, 'life' is one among a whole series of discredited totalities. We are invited to think small rather than big – ironically, at just the point when some of those out to destroy Western civilization are doing exactly the opposite. In the conflict between Western capitalism and radical Islam, a paucity of belief squares up to an excess of it. The West finds itself faced with a full-blooded metaphysical onslaught at just the historical point that it has, so to speak, philosophically disarmed. As far as belief goes, postmodernism prefers to travel light: it has beliefs, to be sure, but it does not have faith.

Even 'meaning' becomes a suspect term for postmodern thinkers like the French philosopher Gilles Deleuze. It assumes that one thing can represent or stand in for another, an assumption which is felt by some to be *passé*. The very idea of interpretation thus comes under assault. Things are just baldly themselves, rather than enigmatic signs of something else. What you see is what you get. Meaning and interpretation imply hidden messages and mechanisms, depths stacked beneath surfaces; but for postmodern thought, this whole surface/depth model smacks of an old-fashioned metaphysics. It is the same with the self, which is no longer a matter of secret folds and interior depths but is now open to view, a decentred network rather than a mysteriously elusive spirit.

This was not true of the pre-modern way of interpreting the world which we know as allegory. For allegory, things do not carry their meanings on their faces; instead, they must be grasped as signs of some underlying 'text' or latent truth, usually of a moral or religious kind. For St Augustine, to attend to objects in themselves reflects a carnal, fallen mode of existence; instead, we must read them semiotically, as pointing beyond themselves to the divine text which is the universe. Semiotics and salvation go hand in hand. The thought of the modern period breaks with this model in one sense while remaining faithful to it in another. Meaning is no longer a spiritual essence buried beneath the surface of things. But it still needs to be dug out, since the world does not spontaneously disclose it. One name for this excavatory enterprise is science, which on a certain view of it seeks to reveal the invisible laws and mechanisms by which things operate. There are still depths, but what is at work in them now is Nature rather than divinity.

Postmodernism then pushes this secularization one step further. As long as we still have depths, essences, and foundations, it insists, we are still in the awesome presence of the Almighty. We have not really killed and buried God at all. We have simply given him a series of majestic new names, like Nature, Man, Reason, History, Power, Desire, and so on. Rather than dismantling the whole outdated apparatus of metaphysics and theology, we have simply given it a new content. Only by breaking with the whole notion of 'deep' meaning, which will always tempt us to chase the chimera of the Meaning of meanings, can we be free. Not, to be sure, free to be ourselves, for we have also dismantled the metaphysical essence known as the self. Quite who is to be set free by this project, then, remains something of a mystery. It may also be that even postmodernism, with its aversion to absolute foundations, secretly smuggles such an absolute into the argument. It is not, to be sure, God or Reason or History, but it behaves in just such a bottom-line sort of way. Like these other absolutes, it is impossible to delve beneath it. For postmodernism, this is known as Culture.

***

Meaning-of-life queries, when launched on a grand scale, tend to arise at times when taken-for-granted roles, beliefs, and conventions are plunged into crisis. Perhaps it is not accidental that the most distinguished works of tragedy tend to spring up at these moments as well. This is not to deny that the meaning-of-life question may be a permanently valid one. But it is surely not irrelevant to the arguments of Heidegger's *Being and Time* that the book was written in just such a period of historical tumult, appearing as it did in the wake of the First World War. Jean-Paul Sartre's *Being and Nothingness*, which also explores such momentous issues, was published in the midst of the Second World War; while existentialism in general, with its sense of the absurdity of human life, flourished in the decades which followed it. Maybe all men and women ponder the meaning of life; but some, for good historical reasons, are driven to ponder it more urgently than others.

If you are forced to inquire on a large scale into the meaning of existence, it is a fair bet that things have come unstuck. Inquiring into the meaning of one's own existence is a different matter, since one might claim that such self-reflection is integral to the business of living a fulfilled life. Someone who has never asked herself how her life is going, and whether it might go better, would seem peculiarly lacking in self-awareness. In which case, it is likely that there are several areas in which her life is not in fact going as well as it might. The very fact that she does not ask herself how things stand with her life suggests that they do not stand as well as they should. If your life is rolling along wonderfully well, one reason for this is probably that you brood from time to time on whether it needs tinkering with or transforming.

In any case, being aware of the fact that you are doing fine is likely to enhance your sense of well-being; and it seems pointless not to add this agreeable bonus to your general state of contentment. It is not true, in other words, that you're only happy if you don't know it. For this naively Romantic view, self-reflection is always fatally stymieing. It is what one might call the high-wire-act-across-an-abyss theory of life: think about it and you instantly come a cropper. But knowing how things stand with you is a necessary condition for knowing whether to try and change them or to keep them more or less as they are. Knowledge is an aid to happiness rather than its antagonist.

To ask about the meaning of human existence as such, however, suggests that we may have collectively lost our way, however we happen to be faring as individuals. Somewhere around 1870 or 1880 in Britain, certain central Victorian certainties on the question began to unravel; so that, say, Thomas Hardy and Joseph Conrad pose the meaning-of-life question with an urgency impossible to imagine in the case of William Thackeray and Anthony Trollope. Or, before these authors, Jane Austen. Of course artists had raised the question before 1870, but rarely as part of a whole *culture* of questioning. By the early decades of the twentieth century, this culture, with its attendant ontological anxieties, had taken the form of modernism. It is a current which was to produce some of the most eminent literary art the West has ever witnessed. With the challenging of almost every traditional value, belief, and institution, the conditions were now ripe for art to pose the most searching questions about the fate of Western culture as such, and beyond that the destiny of humanity itself. No doubt some dreary-minded vulgar Marxist might discern a relation between this cultural upheaval and the late Victorian economic depression, the outbreak of global imperialist warfare in 1916, the Bolshevik Revolution, the rise of fascism, the *inter bellum* economic slump, the emergence of Stalinism, the outbreak of genocide, and the like. We ourselves prefer to confine our speculations less vulgarly to the life of the mind.

This fertile, turbulent strain of thought had a late backwash, as we have seen, in existentialism; but by the 1950s it was generally on the ebb. It surfaced for a late efflorescence in the countercultures of the 1960s; but by the mid-1970s such spiritual ambitions were on the wane, curtailed in the West by an increasingly harsh, pragmatic political climate. Post-structuralism, and then postmodernism, dismissed all attempts to reflect on human life as a whole as disreputably 'humanist' – or indeed as the kind of 'totalizing' theory which led straight to the death camps of the totalitarian state. There was now no such thing as humanity or human life to be contemplated. There were simply differences, specific cultures, local situations.

One reason why the twentieth century brooded on the meaning of existence more agonizedly than most epochs may be because it held human life so appallingly cheap. It was by far the bloodiest epoch on historical record, with millions of unnecessary deaths. If life is so drastically devalued in practice, one might well expect its meaning to be questioned in theory. But there is a more general issue here as well. It is typical of the modern era that what one might call the symbolic dimension of human life is pushed steadily to the margins. Within this dimension, three areas have traditionally been vital: religion, culture, and sexuality. All three of these areas became less central to public life as the modern age unfolded. In pre-modern societies, they belonged for the most part to the public sphere as well as to the private one. Religion was not just a question of personal conscience and individual salvation; it was also a matter of state power, public rituals, and national ideologies. As a key component of international politics, it shaped the destiny of nations all the way from civil wars to dynastic marriages. There are ominous signs that our own period may be reverting to this situation in certain respects.

As for culture, the artist was less a solitary, alienated figure lounging in some raffish bohemian café than a public functionary with an ordained role in the tribe, clan, or court. If he was not in the pay of the Church, he might be hired by the state or some powerful upper-class patron. Artists were rather less inclined to mull over the meaning of life when they had just received a lucrative commission to compose a Requiem Mass. Besides, the question was largely settled for them by their religious faith. Sexuality, then as now, was a matter of erotic love and personal fulfilment. But it was also locked more deeply into the institutions of kinship, inheritance, class, property, power, and status than it is for most of us today.

This is not to idealize the good old days. Religion, art, and sexuality may have been more central to public affairs than they are today; but they could also act as the obedient handmaidens of political power, and for much the same reasons. Once they were able to get out from under such power, they could enjoy a degree of freedom and autonomy that they had never dreamt of before. Yet the price of this freedom was high. These symbolic activities continued to perform important public roles; but in general they were increasingly relegated to the private sphere, where they were really nobody's business but one's own.

How is this relevant to the meaning-of-life question? The answer is that these were exactly the areas to which men and women had traditionally turned when they inquired about the sense and value of their existence. Love, religious faith, and the preciousness of one's kin and culture: it was hard to find more fundamental reasons for living than these. In fact, a great many people over the centuries have been ready to die, or prepared to kill, in their name. People turned to these values all the more eagerly as the public domain itself became increasingly drained of meaning. Fact and value seemed to have split apart, leaving the former a public affair and the latter a private one.

Capitalist modernity, so it appeared, had landed us with an economic system which was almost purely instrumental. It was a way of life dedicated to power, profit, and the business of material survival, rather than to fostering the values of human sharing and solidarity. The political realm was more a question of management and manipulation than of the communal shaping of a common life. Reason itself had been debased to mere self-interested calculation. As for morality, this, too, had become an increasingly private affair, more relevant to the bedroom than the boardroom. Cultural life had grown more important in one sense, burgeoning into a whole industry or branch of material production. In another sense, however, it had dwindled to the window-dressing of a social order which had exceedingly little time for anything it could not price or measure. Culture was now largely a matter of how to keep people harmlessly distracted when they were not working.

Yet there was an irony here. The more culture, religion, and sexuality were forced to act as substitutes for fading public value, the less they were able to do so. The more meaning was concentrated in the symbolic realm, the more that realm was twisted out of true by the pressures that this exerted on it. As a result, all three areas of symbolic life began to exhibit pathological symptoms. Sexuality grew into an exotic obsession. It was one of the few sources of sensationalism left in a jaded world. Sexual shock and outrage stood in for a missing political militancy. Art became similarly inflated in value. For the aestheticist movement, it was now nothing less than a model of how to live. For some modernists, art represented the last fragile dwelling-place of human value in human civilization – a civilization upon which art itself had disdainfully turned its back. Yet this was true only of the work of art's form. Since its content inevitably reflected the reified world around it, it could provide no lasting source of redemption.

Meanwhile, the more religion loomed up as an alternative to the steady haemorrhaging of public meaning, the more it was driven into various ugly forms of fundamentalism. Or if not that, then

2. A 'New Age' gathering at Stonehenge

into New Ageist claptrap. Spirituality, in short, became either rock-hard or soggy. The meaning-of-life question was now in the hands of the gurus and spiritual masseurs, the technologists of piped contentment, and chiropractors of the psyche. With the correct techniques, you could now be guaranteed to shed the flab of meaninglessness in as little as a month. Celebrities whose minds had been addled by adulation turned to Kabbala and Scientology. They were inspired in this by the banal misconception that spirituality must surely be something outlandish and esoteric, rather than practical and material. After all, it was the material, in the shape of private jets and hordes of minders, that they were trying (mentally, at least) to escape from.

For these types, the spiritual was simply the flip side of the material. It was a domain of manufactured mystery which might compensate for the futility of worldly fame. The woollier it was – the less it resembled the soulless calculations of one's agents and accountants – the more meaningful it seemed to be. If everyday life was deficient in meaning, then it would have to be artificially supplemented with the stuff. It could be laced from time to time with a dash of astrology or necromancy, as one might add vitamin pills to one's daily diet. Studying the secrets of the ancient Egyptians made a pleasant change from the tiresome business of finding yourself yet another fifty-bedroom mansion. Besides, since spirituality was all in the mind, it did not require of you any inconvenient sort of action, such as freeing yourself from the burden of running your mansions by giving away large amounts of money to the homeless.

There is another aspect to the story. If the symbolic realm was split off from the public one, it was also invaded by it. Sexuality was packaged as a profitable commodity in the marketplace, while culture meant for the most part profit-hungry mass media. Art was a matter of money, power, status, cultural capital. Cultures were now exotically packaged and peddled by the tourist industry. Even religion turned itself into a profitable industry, as

3. American TV evangelist Jerry Falwell in full fundamentalist flight

TV evangelists conned the pious and gullible poor out of their hard-earned dollars. We had been landed, then, with the worst of both worlds. The places where meaning had traditionally been in most plentiful supply no longer really impinged much on the public world; yet they had also been aggressively colonized by its commercial forces, and so had become part of the leakage of meaning which they had once sought to resist. The now privatized domain of symbolic life had been hassled into delivering more than it decently could. As a result, it was becoming harder to find meaning even in the private sphere. Fiddling while civilization burnt, or cultivating one's garden while history crumbled around you, no longer appeared to be such feasible options as they had been before.

In our own time, one of the most popular, influential branches of the culture industry is unquestionably sport. If you were to ask what provides some meaning in life nowadays for a great many people, especially men, you could do worse than reply 'Football'. Not many of them, perhaps, would be willing to admit as much; but sport, and in Britain football in particular, stands in for all those noble causes – religious faith, national sovereignty, personal honour, ethnic identity – for which, over the centuries, people have been prepared to go to their deaths. Sport involves tribal loyalties and rivalries, symbolic rituals, fabulous legends, iconic heroes, epic battles, aesthetic beauty, physical fulfilment, intellectual satisfaction, sublime spectaculars, and a profound sense of belonging. It also provides the human solidarity and physical immediacy which television does not. Without these values, a good many lives would no doubt be pretty empty. It is sport, not religion, which is now the opium of the people. Indeed, in the world of Christian and Islamic fundamentalism, religion is less the opium of the people than the crack of the masses.

The sham swamis and phoney sages of our time stand in for various more conventional gods who have failed. Philosophers, for example, seem to have been reduced to no more than white-coated

4. The agony and the ecstasy: a sports fan

technicians of language. It is true that the idea of the philosopher as a guide to the meaning of life is a popular misconception. Even so, one might expect them to do rather more than attempt to dissuade people from leaping out of windows by pointing out that the grammar of 'nothing matters' differs from that of 'nothing chatters'.[8] At the same time, theology had been discredited by creeping secularization, as well as by the crimes and follies of the churches. A positivist sociology and behaviourist psychology, along with a visionless political science, completed the betrayal of the intelligentsia. The more the humanities were harnessed to the needs of the economy, the more they abandoned the business of investigating fundamental questions; so the more the Tarot touts, pyramid pushers, avatars of Atlantis, and detoxicators of the soul rushed to fill their place. The Meaning of Life was now a lucrative industry. Books with titles like *Metaphysics for Merchant Bankers* were eagerly devoured. Men and women who were disenchanted with a world obsessed with making money turned to the purveyors of spiritual truth, who made a lot of money out of purveying it.

Why else should the meaning-of-life question raise its head in the era of modernity? Partly, one suspects, because the problem with modern life is that there is too much meaning as well as too little. Modernity is the epoch in which we come to blows over all the most fundamental moral and political questions. In the modern period, then, there have been a great many rival contenders battling it out in the meaning-of-life arena, each unable to deliver a knock-out blow to the others. This means that any one solution to the problem is bound to appear dubious, since there are so many seductive alternatives to hand. We find ourselves here, then, in something of a vicious circle. Once traditional beliefs begin to crumble in the face of historical crisis, the meaning-of-life question tends to thrust itself to the fore. But the very fact that the

---

[8] The Oxford philosopher Gilbert Ryle once claimed that he had argued a student out of suicide by explaining to him this distinction.

question is now so prominent provokes a wide range of responses to it; and this bewildering diversity of solutions then serves to diminish the credibility of any one of them. Feeling it important to raise the meaning-of-life question, then, is a sign that it is going to be hard to answer it.

In this situation, it is always possible for some to find the meaning of life, or at least a sizeable chunk of it, in the very diversity of views on the subject. People who feel this way are generally known as liberals, though nowadays some of them are also known as postmodernists. For them, what matters is not so much a definitive answer to the meaning-of-life question as the fact that there are so many exotically varied ways of answering it. In fact, the freedom which this signifies may itself be the most precious meaning we shall ever stumble upon. What some see as hopeless fragmentation, then, others regard as exhilarating liberation.

For most of those in hot pursuit of the meaning of life, what counts above all is the quarry. For liberals and postmodernists, however, what matters is the delightful din of the conversation itself, which in their view is probably as much meaning as we shall ever unearth. The meaning of life consists in the search for the meaning of life. A good many liberals tend to prefer questions to answers, since they regard answers as unduly restrictive. Questions are free-floating, whereas answers are not. The point is to have an inquiring mind, not to snap it shut with some drearily determinate solution. It is true that this approach does not work too well with questions like 'How can we get the food to them before they starve?', or 'Would this be an effective way of preventing racist murders?' But perhaps liberals have higher kinds of questions in mind.

Liberal pluralism, however, has its limits. For some of the answers proposed to the meaning-of-life question are not only in conflict with each other, but are mutually contradictory. You may hold that the meaning of life lies in caring for the vulnerable, whereas I may maintain that it lies in bullying as many sick, defenceless creatures as I can lay my hands on. Though we might both be wrong, we cannot both be right. Even the liberal must be rigorously exclusive here, ruling out any solution (the building of a totalitarian state, for example) which might undermine his or her commitment to freedom and plurality. Freedom must not be allowed to destroy its own foundations, even though radicals would argue that in capitalist conditions it does so every day of the week.

Pluralism has its limits in this sense, too, that if there is such a thing as *the* meaning of life, it cannot be different for each of us. I can say 'The meaning of my life is drinking as much whisky as is compatible with just about being able to crawl'; but I cannot say 'The meaning of life for me is drinking a lot of whisky', unless this is just another way of making the former claim. It would be rather like saying 'The colour of snow for me is turquoise tinged with magenta', or 'The meaning of "skittles" for me is "water lilies"'. Meaning cannot just be whatever I decide. If life does have a meaning, then that is its meaning for you, me, and everyone else, whatever meaning we might think it has or would like it to have. Anyway, it may be that life has a number of meanings. Why should we imagine that it has only one? Just as we can assign it many different meanings, so it may have a variety of innate meanings, if it has innate meanings at all. Perhaps there are several different purposes at work in it, some of them mutually contradictory. Or perhaps life changes its purpose from time to time, just as we do. We should not suppose that the given or innate must always be fixed and singular. What if life does indeed have a purpose, but one completely at odds with our own projects? It may be that life has a meaning, but that the vast majority of men and women who have ever lived have been mistaken about what it is. If religion is false, then this is in fact the case.

Many of the readers of this book, however, are likely to be as sceptical of the phrase 'the meaning of life' as they are of Santa Claus. It seems a quaint sort of notion, at once homespun and

5. Michael Palin as an unctuous Anglican vicar in the Monty Python film, 'The Meaning of Life'.

portentous, fit for satirical mauling by the Monty Python team.[9]
A great many educated people in the West today, at least outside
the astonishingly religious United States, believe that life is an
accidental evolutionary phenomenon which has no more intrinsic
meaning than a fluctuation of the breeze or a rumble in the gut.
The fact that it has no given meaning, however, then clears the
ground for individual men and women to make what sense of it
they may. If our lives have meaning, it is something with which
we manage to invest them, not something with which they come
ready equipped.

On this theory, we are self-authoring animals, who do not need
to have our narratives written for us by an abstraction known as
Life. For Nietzsche or Oscar Wilde, we could all (had we but the
daring) be supreme artists of ourselves, clay in our own hands,
waiting to fashion ourselves into some exquisitely unique shape.
The conventional wisdom on this matter, I take it, is that the
meaning of life is not prefabricated but constructed; and that each
of us can do this in very different ways. No doubt there is a good
deal of truth in this case; but because it is also rather bland and
boring, I want to put it under pressure in these pages. Some of
this book, then, will be devoted to interrogating this view of the
meaning of life as a kind of private enterprise, in order to see how
far it holds up.

[9] There is another, non-Pythonesque film called *The Meaning of Life*, which
I once saw in the Mormon Temple in Salt Lake City. Unfortunately, I have
completely forgotten what it claimed the meaning of life to be, partly because of
my surprise that it only lasted about four minutes.

Chapter 2
The problem of meaning

'What is the meaning of life?' is one of those rare questions in which almost every word is problematic. This even includes the first one, since for the countless millions of people who are religious believers, the meaning of life is not a what but a Who. A dedicated Nazi might well have agreed with this after his own fashion, finding the meaning of life in the person of Adolf Hitler. The meaning of life may only be revealed to us at the end of time, in the form of a Messiah who seems to be taking his time arriving. Or the universe might be an atom in the thumbnail of some cosmic giant.

The really contentious word, however, is 'meaning'. We tend nowadays to believe that the meaning of a word is its use in a specific form of life; but the word 'meaning' itself has a whole number of such uses. Here are some of them:

> *Poisson* means 'fish'.
> Did you mean to strangle him?
> Those clouds mean rain.
> When she referred to 'a flea-bitten, geriatric donkey', did she mean
>   the one in the paddock over there?
> What is the meaning of this disgraceful affair?
> I meant you, not her.
> Lavender-scented bath soap means a lot to him.

The Ukranians clearly mean business.

This portrait is meant to be priceless.

Lavinia means well, but Julius probably doesn't.

When the deceased asked the waiter for *poison*, could he by any
chance have meant *poisson*?

Their encounter seemed almost meant.

His rages don't mean a thing.

Cordelia was meant to return the corkscrew by Sunday lunchtime.

These uses of the word could be said to fall into three categories.
One is to do with intending something or having it in mind; in
fact, the word 'meaning' is etymologically related to the word
'mind'. Another category concerns the idea of signifying, while the
third runs the first two categories together by indicating the act of
intending or having it in mind to signify something.

'Did you mean to strangle him?' is clearly an inquiry about your
intentions, or what you had in your mind at the time, and so is 'I
meant you, not her'. For their encounter to seem somehow 'meant'
is for it to appear mysteriously intended, perhaps by destiny.
'Lavinia means well' means that she has good intentions, though
they probably don't always get translated into effective action.
'Cordelia was meant to return the corkscrew' means that we had
it in mind (or expected) that she would. 'The Ukranians clearly
mean business' is a statement about their resolute purposes or
intentions. 'This portrait is meant to be priceless' is more or less
synonymous with 'It is thought to be priceless', meaning that this
is the 'mind' of those in the know. This does not quite pick up the
notion of intending. But most of the other examples do.

By contrast, 'Those clouds mean rain', and 'Lavender-scented soap
means a lot to him' do not refer to intentions or states of mind.
The clouds do not 'intend to signify' rain; they just do signify
it. Since lavender-scented soap has no mind of its own, to say
that it means a lot to someone is simply to say that it signifies a
lot. The same goes for 'What is the meaning of this disgraceful

34

affair?', which is asking about what the affair signifies. Not, notice, what the individuals involved in it are trying to signify, but the significance of the situation itself. 'His rages don't mean a thing' means that they do not signify anything, but not necessarily that he is not trying to signify anything by them. It is not a question of his intentions. The third category, as we have seen, refers not just to intending, or just to signifying, but to the act of intending to signify something. This includes questions like 'What did she mean by a flea-bitten, geriatric donkey?', or 'Did he really mean *poisson*?'

It is important to distinguish between meaning as a given signification and meaning as an act which intends to signify something. Both meanings can be found in a sentence like 'I meant (intended) to ask for *poisson*, but the word I actually came out with signifies poison'. 'What do you mean?' means 'What do you have it in mind to signify?', whereas 'What does the word mean?' asks what signifying value it has within a given linguistic system. These two different senses of 'meaning' are sometimes referred to by students of language as meaning as *act* and meaning as *structure*. As far as the latter case goes, the meaning of a word is a function of a linguistic structure – so that the word 'fish' gets its meaning by the place it has in a system of language, the relations it has with other words within this system, and so on. If, then, life has a meaning, it may be one which we ourselves actively give it, along the lines of investing a set of black marks on a page with some sort of sense; or it may be a meaning which it has anyway despite our own activity, which is rather more parallel to the idea of meaning as structure or function.

Pressed a bit further, however, these two senses of 'meaning' are not so distinct after all. Indeed, you can imagine a kind of chicken-and-egg relation between them. 'Fish' means a scaly aquatic creature, but only because this is the way the word has been used by countless number of English-language speakers. The word itself can be seen as a kind of repository or sedimentation of a whole series of historical acts. Conversely, however, I can only use the word 'fish' to refer to scaly aquatic creatures because this is what the word signifies within the structure of my language.

Words are not just dead husks waiting to have meaning breathed into them by live speakers. What I can mean (in the sense of intend to say) is constrained by the meanings I find ready to hand in the language I speak. I cannot 'mean' a series of words which are entirely senseless, though as we shall see in a moment I can signify something by it. Nor can I intend to say something which lies entirely outside the scope of my language, rather as someone cannot intend to become a brain surgeon if they don't have the concept of brain surgeon in the first place. I cannot just make a word mean what I want it to mean. Even if I conjure up a vivid mental picture of a smoked herring as I pronounce the words 'World Health Organization', the meaning of what I have said is still 'World Health Organization'.

If we think of meaning as the function of a word in a linguistic system, then anyone who has mastered that system can be said to understand the meaning of a word. If someone asks me how I know the meaning of 'the path to perdition', it might be enough to reply that I speak English. But this does not mean that I understand a particular use of the phrase. For it can be used in different circumstances to refer to different things; and to know what it means in *this* sense of the word 'means', I would need to take into account the intended meaning of a particular speaker or speakers in a specific context. I would need, in short, to see how the phrase is being concretely applied; and simply knowing the dictionary meaning of the individual words is not enough here. What a word is referring to or picking out in a particular situation is not always easy to identify. One of the Australian Aboriginal words for 'alcohol' is 'ducking', because Aboriginal people first picked up the word in the context of loyal toasts to 'the king' by their colonial masters.

It would be possible to say of someone: 'I understood his *words*; but I didn't *understand* his words.' I was familiar enough with the significations he was using, but I didn't grasp how he was using them – what he was referring to, what kind of attitude he was implying towards it, what he wanted me to understand by his words, why he wanted me to understand it, and so on. In order to illuminate all this, I would need to put his words back into a specific context; or – what comes to the same thing – I would need to grasp them as part of a narrative. And as far as that goes, being acquainted with the dictionary meaning of the words won't help a great deal. In this latter case, then, we are talking about meaning as an act – as something people do, as a social practice, as the variety of ways, sometimes ambiguous and mutually contradictory, in which they actually deploy a particular sign in a specific form of life.

What light, then, do these different meanings of 'meaning' shed on the question 'What is the meaning of life?' To begin with, 'What is the meaning of life?' is obviously different from 'What is the meaning of "potlatch"?' The first question is asking about the meaning of a phenomenon, while the second is inquiring about the meaning of a word. It is not the word 'life' we find bemusing, but the thing itself. For another thing, we can note that when somebody wails 'My life is meaningless', they do not mean that it makes no sense in the way that *&$£%"* makes no sense. Rather, it is meaningless more in the sense that 'Assuring you most earnestly of our respectful attention at all times, we remain your obliged and devoted servants...' is meaningless. People who find life meaningless are not complaining that they cannot tell what kind of stuff their body is made out of, or that they do not know whether they are in a black hole or under the ocean. Men and women whose lives lack meaning in that sense of the word are psychotic, not just down-hearted. They mean, rather, that their lives lack *significance*. And to lack significance means to lack point, substance, purpose, quality, value, and direction. Such people mean not that they cannot comprehend

37

life, but that they have nothing to live for. It is not that their existence is unintelligible, merely empty. But to know that they are empty requires a fair amount of interpretation, and thus of meaning. 'My life is meaningless' is an existential statement, not a logical one. Someone whose life feels meaningless is more likely to reach for the suicide pills than for the dictionary.

Shakespeare's Macbeth does not have to commit suicide, since his enemy Macduff despatches him to eternity with a sword thrust; but the Scottish usurper ends up in just that despairing state of mind:

> ... Out, out, brief candle!
> Life's but a walking shadow, a poor player,
> That struts and frets his hour upon the stage,
> And then is heard no more; it is a tale
> Told by an idiot, full of sound and fury,
> Signifying nothing.
>
> Act 5, scene 5

The passage is a lot more puzzling than it looks. Macbeth is really complaining about two aspects of life – its transience and its vacuousness – and one can see the connection between the two. Achievements are hollowed out by the fact that they fade away so quickly. Yet the ephemerality of things is not necessarily tragic: it can be seen simply as part of the way they are, with no inevitably doleful implications. If fine dinners fade away, so do tyrants and toothache. Could a human life which had no limit, stretching all the way to infinity, have a significant shape to it? Isn't death in this sense one of the pre-conditions for life having meaning at all? Or could such a life still be meaningful in senses of the term other than 'having a significant shape'? Anyway, if life really is so transitory, why should the very thought of this impel you to make it even more so ('Out, out, brief candle!')?

6. John Gielgud as a terrified Macbeth

Like a dramatic performance, so the lines suggest, human existence does not persist very long. But the image threatens to undermine the thought behind it, since it is in the nature of a play not to last too long. We do not want to sit in the theatre for ever. Why then should the brevity of life not be equally acceptable? Or, for that matter, even more so, since the brevity of life is natural, as a drama is not? Besides, the fact that an actor makes an exit does not invalidate everything she has done or said on-stage. On the contrary, her exit is part of that meaning. She does not just wander off at random. In this sense, too, the theatre image runs counter to the idea that death undercuts our achievements as well as cutting them off.

It is surely no accident that when Shakespeare has to conjure up a negative vision, he offers us the figure of a ham actor. They were, after all, the men most likely to ruin both his reputation and his bank balance. Like a poor player ('poor' meaning perhaps both 'incompetent' and 'to be pitied'), life is senseless because it is stagey, unreal, stuffed full of portentous rhetoric which is really no more than hot air. An actor does not actually 'mean' what he or she says, and neither does life. But isn't this comparison falsifying? Isn't this the 'intend to say' notion of meaning, which as we have seen is only dubiously applicable to life in the first place?

And what of 'a tale told by an idiot'? In one sense, this is rather consoling. Life may be fatuous, but at least it constitutes a tale, which implies some sort of rudimentary structure. It may be garbled, but there is a narrator behind it, even if an imbecilic one. In a BBC television production of the play some years ago, the actor playing Macbeth delivered these final lines not in a broken mumble but in a raging outburst of resentment, bawling them in fury to an overhead camera which was clearly meant to stand in for the Almighty. It was God who was the idiot narrator. As with the Schopenhaurian vision of the world we shall be examining in a moment, there was indeed an author to this monstrous farce, but this did not mean that it added up. On the contrary, it simply lent a sick twist of irony to its absurdity. There is, however, an ambiguity here: is the tale inherently nonsensical, or is it nonsensical because it is recounted by an idiot? Or is it both? The image might imply, perhaps without quite wishing to do so, that life is the kind of thing that *could* make sense, just as the word 'tale' might also be taken to suggest this. How can something literally signify nothing and still be a story?

Like a bombastic speech, life appears to be meaningful but is actually vapid. As with a bungling actor, it pretends to meaning but falls short of it. A swell of signifiers ('full of sound and fury') conceals an absence of signifieds ('signifying nothing'). Like a piece of shoddy rhetoric, life is a matter of flamboyantly filling in the void which is itself. It is deceitful as well as null. So it is bitter disenchantment which is at stake here, as the false king's political ambitions turn to ashes in his mouth. Yet the imagery, once again, is partly deceptive. Actors, after all, are as real as anyone else. They genuinely do create fictions, and the stage on which they do so is equally solid. (The metaphor, perhaps contrary to its own intentions, implies that the world (or stage) is unreal as well as the actor, whereas you could always claim that human life is a sham but that its material environs are not.) Actors who are 'heard no more' are in the wings, not in the graveyard.

At least two notions of meaninglessness are at work in the passage. One of them is existential: human existence is a void or empty farce. There are meanings in plenty, but they are specious. The other notion we might call semantic, implying as it does that life is senseless in the way that a piece of gibberish is. This is the tale told by an idiot, signifying nothing. Life is unintelligible as well as inane. Strictly speaking, though, you cannot run both meanings in tandem. For if existence really were unintelligible, it would be impossible to pass moral judgements on it, such as the judgement that it is empty of significance. It would be like dismissing as nonsense a word from a foreign language which we could not even translate.

If the meaning-of-life question is not like trying to make sense of a piece of nonsense, neither is it the same as 'What is the meaning of *Nacht* in English?' It is not as though we are asking for the equivalent in one system of a term in another system, as we are when we ask for a translation of this kind. In *The Hitchhiker's Guide to the Galaxy*, Douglas Adams writes famously of a computer called Deep Thought which is asked to work out the ultimate answer to the universe, takes seven and a half million years to do so, and finally comes up with the answer 42. Another, larger computer then has to be built, to figure out what the actual question was. One is reminded of the American poet Gertrude Stein, who was rumoured on her deathbed to have asked over and over again 'What is the answer?', before finally murmuring 'But what is the question?' A question about a question posed while hovering on the brink of nothingness seems a suitable symbol of the modern condition.

What is amusing about Deep Thought's '42' is not just the bathos of it, a notion we shall be looking at a bit later. It is also the absurdity of supposing that '42' could even count as an answer to the question, which would be like imagining that 'Two packets of plain crisps and a pickled egg' could count as an answer to 'When is the sun likely to pack up?' We are dealing here with what philosophers call a category mistake, like asking how many emotions it takes to stop a truck, which is one reason why it is funny. Another reason why it is funny is that we are given an unequivocal solution to a question which many people have yearned to have answered, yet it is a solution with which we can do absolutely nothing. '42' simply does not mesh with anything. It is not a response we can find a use for. It sounds like a precise, authoritative solution to a problem, but it is really just like saying 'Broccoli'.

Another comic aspect of the answer is that it treats the question 'What is the meaning of life?' as though it were the same kind of question as 'What is the meaning of *Nacht*?' Just as a relationship of equivalence holds between the German *Nacht* and English 'night', so Adams's comic fantasy suggests that life can be translated into another signifying system (this time a numerical rather than verbal one), with the result that you come up with a number which signifies the meaning of life. Or it is as though life is a kind of riddle, conundrum, or cryptogram which can be deciphered like a crossword clue to produce this snappy answer. Lurking behind the joke is the idea of life as a problem in the sense of a mathematical problem, which has a solution in the way that such problems do. It runs together for comic effect two different senses of the word 'problem': a crossword or mathematical puzzle and a problematic phenomenon such as human existence. It is as though life could be decoded in a *Eureka*-type moment, allowing a single momentous word – Power, Guinness, Love, Sex, Chocolate – to flash for an enthralling moment across our consciousness.

Could the word 'meaning' in the phrase 'the meaning of life' have something like the sense it does in the 'what someone intends to signify' category? Surely not, unless (for example) you believe that life is the utterance of God, a sign or discourse in which he is trying to communicate something significant to us. The great Irish philosopher Bishop Berkeley believed just this. In that case, the meaning of life refers to an *act* of meaning – to whatever significance it is that God (or the Life Force, or the *Zeitgeist*) intends to convey by it. But what if one believes in none of these august entities? Does this mean that life must be meaningless?

Not necessarily. Marxists, for instance, are usually atheists, but they believe that human life, or what they would prefer to call 'history', has a meaning in the sense of displaying a significant pattern. Those championing the so-called Whig theory of history, which reads the human narrative as the steady unfolding of freedom and enlightenment, also see human life as forming a significant pattern, though not one that any Supreme Being smuggled into it. It is true that these grand narratives are nowadays out of fashion; but they make the point, even so, that it is possible to believe in the meaningfulness of life without claiming that this meaning has been ascribed to it by an intending subject. Meaning in the sense of significant pattern is not, to be sure, the same sense of the word 'meaning' as the act of intending to say something, or meaning in the sense that a red light signifies 'stop'. Yet it is surely one thing we occasionally mean by 'meaning'. If there were no significant patterns in human life, even though no single individual intends them, whole areas of the humanities such as sociology and anthropology would grind to a halt. A demographer may remark that the distribution of population in a certain region 'makes sense', even though nobody living in that region may actually be aware of this pattern.

It is possible, then, to believe that there is a significant narrative embedded in reality, even though it has no superhuman source. The novelist George Eliot, for example, was not a religious believer; but a novel like *Middlemarch*, like many a realist work of literature, assumes that there is a meaningful design inherent in history itself. The task of the classical realist writer is less to invent a fable than to flesh out the hidden logic of a story which is immanent in reality. Contrast this, then, with a modernist author like Joyce, for whom a pattern has to be projected into the universe rather than excavated from it. Joyce's novel *Ulysses* is intricately organized all the way through by the Greek myth referred to in its title; but part of the joke is that any other myth would probably have served just as well to smuggle a semblance of order into a contingent, chaotic world.

In this rather loose sense of 'meaningful' as 'revealing a significant design', we can speak of the meaning of something without assuming that this meaning has an author; and this is a point worth noting when it comes to the meaning of life. The cosmos may not have been consciously designed, and is almost certainly not struggling to say anything, but it is not just chaotic either. On the contrary, its underlying laws reveal a beauty, symmetry, and economy which are capable of moving scientists to tears. The idea that the world is either given meaning by God, or is utterly random and absurd, is a false antithesis. Even those who do happen to believe that God is the ultimate meaning of life do not have to hold that without this divine bedrock there would be no coherent meaning at all.

Religious fundamentalism is the neurotic anxiety that without a Meaning of meanings, there is no meaning at all. It is simply the flip side of nihilism. Underlying this assumption is the house-of-cards view of life: flick away the one at the bottom, and the whole fragile structure comes fluttering down. Someone who thinks this way is simply the prisoner of a metaphor. In fact, a great many believers reject this view. No sensitive, intelligent religious believer imagines that non-believers are bound to be mired in total absurdity. Nor are they bound to believe that because there is a God, the meaning of life becomes luminously clear. On the contrary, some of those with religious faith believe that God's presence makes the world more mysteriously unfathomable, not less. If he does have a purpose, it is remarkably impenetrable. God is not in that sense the answer to a problem. He tends to thicken things rather than render them self-evident.

The philosopher Immanuel Kant, in considering both natural organisms and works of art, wrote of them in his *Critique of Judgement* as displaying what he called 'purposiveness without purpose'. The human body does not have a purpose; yet one can speak of its various parts as having a 'meaning' in terms of their place within the whole. And these are not significances which we ourselves decide on. Nobody designed the human foot, and it would no doubt be an abuse of language to speak of its 'purpose' as being to help us kick, walk, and run. But the foot has a function within the whole organism of the body, so that it would make sense for someone ignorant of human anatomy to ask about its significance. Just as one thing we mean by 'meaning' is the function of a word within a system, so we can say with only a modest straining of language that the foot is meaningful within the body as a whole. It is not just a random flap or hinge on the end of your leg.

To take another example: it would not be all that eccentric to ask 'What is the meaning of that noise?' as you hear the wind gusting eerily through the trees. The wind is not trying to express anything, to be sure; but its sound 'signifies' even so. To satisfy the speaker's curiosity or allay his alarm, we recount a little narrative about air pressure, acoustics, and so on. Once again, this is not a significance which we ourselves get to decide on. It would even be possible to say of a random pattern of pebbles that they mean something – that they accidentally spell out, say, the phrase 'All Power to the Soviets', even though nobody put them there with this purpose.[10]

Something which comes about accidentally, as life seems to have done, can still exhibit a design. 'Accidental' does not mean 'unintelligible'. Car accidents are not unintelligible. They are not freakish events entirely without rhyme or reason, but the consequence of specific causes. It is just that this consequence was not intended by those involved. A process may seem accidental at the time but fall into a significant pattern retrospectively. This is more or less how Hegel viewed the history of the world. It may seem pretty meaningless while we are living it, but for Hegel it all makes perfect sense when, so to speak, the *Zeitgeist* looks back over its shoulder and casts an admiring eye upon what it has created. In Hegel's eyes, even the blunders and blind alleyways of history contribute in the end to this grand design. The opposite view is the one implicit in the old joke 'My life is full of fascinating characters, but I don't seem to be able to work out the plot'. It seems meaningful from one moment to the next, but it doesn't appear to stack up.

---

[10] A claim denied by the philosopher Roger Scruton in his *Modern Philosophy* (London, 1994), 251. The phrase Scruton himself uses is not 'All Power to the Soviets' but 'God is dead' – an unconsciously significant choice, given that the Nietzschean proclamation of the death of God or ultimate donor of meaning is thought to unleash interpretative anarchy on the world. My own example is no doubt just as revealing.

How else can we think about unintended meanings? An artist might paint the word 'pig' on her canvas not to communicate the concept 'pig' – not to 'mean' it, but simply because she is entranced by the shape of the word. Yet the shape would mean 'pig' all the same. The opposite of this would be a writer who inserted great wads of gobbledygook into his work. If this had an artistic purpose, we might say that the words had meaning in the sense of having significance, even if they are literally senseless. They might signify, for instance, a Dadaist assault on the suburban illusion of the stability of meaning. The author would 'intend' something by this act, even if what he 'meant to say' could only be conveyed by words which made no sense within his language system.

We speak of the complex network of meanings of a Shakespeare play without always supposing that Shakespeare was holding these meanings in his head at the exact moment of writing the words down. How could any poet of such prodigal imaginative fertility keep in mind all the possible connotations of his meanings? To say 'This is a possible meaning of the work' is sometimes to say that this is what the work can be plausibly interpreted to mean. What the author actually 'had in mind' may be completely beyond recovery, even for himself. Many writers have had the experience of being shown patterns of meaning in their work which they did not mean to put there. And what of unconscious meanings, which are by definition not deliberately intended? 'I really do think with my pen', Wittgenstein observes, 'because my head often knows nothing about what my hand is writing.'[11]

***

Just as it is possible to believe that something – even 'life' – may have a significant design or direction which nobody intended, so you can believe that human existence is meaningless and chaotic, but that this was actually intended. It may be the product of

[11] Ludwig Wittgenstein, *Culture and Value* (Chicago, 1984), 17e.

a malevolent Fate or Will. This, roughly speaking, is the view of the German philosopher Arthur Schopenhauer, a thinker so unremittingly gloomy that his work, quite unintentionally, represents one of the great comic masterpieces of Western thought. (There is even something comic about his name, combining as it does the noble, mouth-filling 'Schopenhauer' with the rather more commonplace 'Arthur'.) In Schopenhauer's view, the whole of reality (and not just human life) is the passing product of what he terms the Will. The Will, which is a voracious, implacable force, has a kind of intentionality about it; but if it generates everything there is, it is for no more reputable reason than to keep itself in business. By reproducing reality, the Will serves to reproduce itself, though to absolutely no purpose. So there is indeed an essence or central dynamic to life; but it is a horrific rather than an exalted truth, one which gives birth to havoc, chaos, and perpetual misery. Not all grand narratives are starry-eyed ones.

Because the Will is purely self-determining, it has its end entirely in itself, like a malevolent caricature of the Almighty. And this means that it simply uses us and the rest of Creation for its own inscrutable purposes. We may believe that our lives have value and meaning; but the truth is that we exist simply as the helpless instruments of the Will's blind, futile self-reproduction. In order to achieve this, however, the Will must fool us into supposing that our lives indeed have meaning; and it does so by evolving in us a clumsy mechanism of self-deception known as consciousness, which permits us the illusion of having ends and values of our own. It dupes us into believing that its own appetites are ours too. In this sense, all consciousness in Schopenhauer's eyes is false consciousness. Just as it was once said of language that it exists so that we can conceal our thoughts from others, so consciousness exists to conceal from us the utter futility of our existence. Otherwise, confronted with the panorama of carnage and sterility known as human history, we would surely do away with ourselves. Even suicide, however, represents a cunning triumph of the Will,

7. Arthur Schopenhauer, as grim as his vision of life

whose own immortality is dramatically demonstrated by contrast with the mortality of its human puppets.

Schopenhauer, then, belongs to a lineage of thinkers for whom false consciousness, far from being a mist to be dispelled by the clear light of reason, is absolutely integral to our existence.

Nietzsche, whose early writings were influenced by Schopenhauer, was another such thinker. 'Truth is ugly', he writes in *The Will to Power*. 'We possess art lest we perish of the truth.'[12] Sigmund Freud was yet another who was profoundly shaped by his pessimistic compatriot. What Schopenhauer names the Will, Freud re-baptizes as Desire. For Freud, fantasy, misperception, and a repression of the Real are constitutive of the self, not accidental to it. Without such saving oblivion, we would never get by. What, then, if there was indeed a meaning to life, but that it was preferable for us not to know it? We tend to assume that discovering the meaning of life would naturally be a worthwhile thing to do, but what if this is a mistake? What if the Real was a monstrosity that would turn us to stone?

We can always ask, after all, why someone should *want* to know the meaning of life. Are they sure that it will help them to live better? After all, men and women have lived superlative lives without apparently being in possession of this secret. Or perhaps they were in possession of the secret of life all along without knowing it. Maybe the meaning of life is something I am doing right now, as simple as breathing, without the faintest awareness of it. What if it is elusive not because it is concealed, but because it is too close to the eyeball to have a clear view of? Perhaps the meaning of life is not some goal to be pursued, or some chunk of truth to be dredged up, but something which is articulated in the act of living itself, or perhaps in a certain way of living. The meaning of a narrative, after all, is not just the 'end' of it, in either sense of the word, but the process of narration itself.

Wittgenstein puts the point well. 'If anyone should think he has solved the problem of life', he writes, 'and feel like telling himself that everything is quite easy now, he can see that he is wrong just by recalling that there was a time when this "solution" had not

---

[12] Friedrich Nietzsche, *The Will to Power* (New York, 1975), 435.

been discovered; but it must have been possible to live *then* too and the solution which has now been discovered seems fortuitous in relation to how things were then.'[13] Behind this sentiment lurks Wittgenstein's conviction that the meaning of life, if there is such a thing, is neither a secret nor a 'solution', ideas which we shall be investigating later. Meanwhile, we can ask once again: what if the meaning of life were something that we should at all costs *not* discover?

This is not the kind of thought which would readily have occurred to the thinkers of the Enlightenment, for whom error was to be courageously combated by truth. As the eighteenth century turns into the nineteenth, however, the notion of the redemptive lie or salutary fiction swims gradually into view. Perhaps human beings would simply perish of the truth, withering beneath its remorseless glare. Maybe fictions and myths are not just errors to be dispelled, but productive illusions which allow us to thrive. Life may be no more than a biological accident, and not even an accident that was waiting to happen; but it has developed in us a random phenomenon known as the mind, which we can use to shield ourselves from the frightful knowledge of our own contingency.

It is as though a homeopathic Nature has kindly furnished us with the cure along with the poison, and both are known as consciousness. We can turn our minds to bleak speculations on the way that Nature seems so indifferent to individual lives in its ruthless concern for the species as a whole. Or we can divert our thoughts to the business of building life-giving mythologies – religion, humanism, and the like – which might assign us some status and significance in this inhospitable universe. Such mythologies may not be true from a scientific viewpoint. But perhaps we have made too much of a fuss of scientific truth, assuming that it is the only brand of truth around.

[13] Wittgenstein, *Culture and Value*, 4e.

Like the humanities in general, such myths can be said to contain their own kind of truth, one which lies more in the consequences they produce than in the propositions they advance. If they allow us to act with a sense of value and purpose, then perhaps they are true enough to be going on with.

By the time we arrive at the work of the twentieth-century Marxist theorist Louis Althusser, this way of thinking has even infiltrated Marxism, with its stern opposition to the false consciousness of ideology. What if ideology, after all, were vitally necessary? What if we need it to persuade ourselves that we are political agents capable of acting autonomously? Marxist theory may be aware that the individual has no great degree of unity or autonomy, or even of reality; but individuals themselves must come to trust that they have, if they are to act effectively. For Althusser, it is the task of socialist ideology to secure this saving illusion. For Freud, much the same is true of the ego, which is actually no more than an offshoot of the unconscious, but which is so organized as to regard the whole world as centred on itself. The ego treats itself as a coherent, independent entity, which psychoanalysis knows to be an illusion; but it is a salutary illusion all the same, without which we would be unable to operate.

It seems, then, that far from speaking of the meaning of life, we might be faced with a choice between meaning and life. What if the truth were destructive of human existence? What if it were an annihilating Dionysian force, as the early Nietzsche considered; a rapacious Will, as in Schopenhauer's sombre speculations; or a devouring, ruthlessly impersonal desire, as for Freud? For the psychoanalytical thinker Jacques Lacan, the human subject can either 'mean' or 'be', but it cannot do both together. Once we enter into language, and thus into our humanity, what one might call the 'truth of the subject', its being-as-such, is divided up into an unending chain of partial meanings. We attain meaning only at the price of a loss of being.

It is with the novelist Joseph Conrad, who felt the influence of both Nietzsche and Schopenhauer, that this vein of thought first entered English writing on a grand scale. As a full-blooded philosophical sceptic, Conrad did not believe that our concepts, values, and ideals have any foundation in a world which is as meaningless as the waves. Even so, there are pressing moral and political reasons why we should behave *as if* they were firmly grounded. If we do not, social anarchy might well be one unwelcome consequence. There is even a sense in which what we believe is less important than the sheer fact of our faith. This brand of formalism then passes on into existentialism, for which it is the fact of being committed, rather than the exact content of our commitments, which is the key to an authentic existence.

The playwright Arthur Miller's protagonists are a case in point. Characters like Willy Loman in *Death of a Salesman*, or Eddie Carbone in *A View from the Bridge*, are committed to a version of their own identities, and of the world around them, which from an objective viewpoint is false. Willy, for example, believes that what counts in life is to be socially respected and economically successful. Yet what matters with these self-blinded figures, as with some of Ibsen's tragic protagonists, is the intensity with which they invest in this commitment. It is the heroic tenacity with which they stay true to their twisted images of themselves that counts in the end, even though it leads them to delusion and death. To live with faith – any old faith, perhaps – is to infuse one's life with significance. On this view, the meaning of life is a question of the style in which you live it, not of its actual content.

It is self-evident to Schopenhauer that only an idiot could imagine that life was worth living. For him, the most fitting emblem of the human enterprise is the shovel-pawed mole:

> To dig strenuously with its enormous shovel-paws is the business
> of its whole life; permanent night surrounds it … what does it
> attain by this course of life that is full of trouble and devoid of

pleasure? Nourishment and procreation, that is, only the means
for continuing and beginning again in the new individual the same
melancholy course.[14]

The whole human project is clearly a ghastly mistake which
should have been called off long ago. Only the obtusely
self-deluded, confronted with the charnel house of history, could
imagine otherwise. The human narrative has been one of such
unrelieved wretchedness that only those conned by the low
cunning of the Will could consider it worth having been born.

There is something ridiculous in Schopenhauer's eyes about
this pompously self-important race of creatures, each of them
convinced of his own supreme value, pursuing some edifying
end which will instantly turn to ashes in his mouth. There is
no grandiose goal to this meaningless sound and fury, only
'momentary gratification, fleeting pleasure conditioned by wants,
much and long suffering, constant struggle, *bellum omnium*,
everything a hunter and everything hunted, pressure, want, need
and anxiety, shrieking and howling; and this goes on in *saecula
saeculorum* or until once again the crust of the planet breaks'.[15] As
far as Schopenhauer can tell, 'no-one has the remotest idea why
the whole tragic-comedy exists, for it has no spectators, and the
actors themselves undergo endless worry with little and merely
negative enjoyment'.[16] The world is simply a futile craving, a
grotesquely bad drama, an immense marketplace or Darwinian
amphitheatre in which life-forms seek to crush the breath out of
each other.

There is, of course, always the company of others; but for
Schopenhauer it is sheer boredom which drives us to seek it out.
As far as the Will is concerned, there is no notable distinction

[14] Arthur Schopenhauer, *The World as Will and Representation* (New York,
1969), ii. 353–4.
[15] Ibid. 354.   [16] Ibid. 357.

between humans and polyps, both alike being instruments of its blankly indifferent dynamic. At the very core of human beings stirs a power – the Will – which is the very stuff of their inner being, yet which is as unfeeling and anonymous as the force which stirs the waves. Subjectivity is what we can least call our own. We bear inside us an inert weight of meaninglessness, as if permanently pregnant with monsters; and this, which is the action of the Will within us, constitutes the very core of our selfhood. Everything is fraught with appetite: human beings are simply walking incarnations of their parents' copulatory instincts, and the whole of this fruitless desiring is founded in lack. 'All *willing*', Schopenhauer writes, 'springs from lack, from deficiency, and thus from suffering.'[17] Desiring is eternal, whereas fulfilment is scanty and sporadic. There can be no end to the fatal infection we know as desire as long as the self endures. Only the selflessness of aesthetic contemplation, along with a kind of Buddhist self-abnegation, can purge us of the astigmatism of wanting, and allow us to see the world for what it is.

There is, needless to say, another story to tell. Yet if Schopenhauer is still well worth reading, it is not only because he confronts the possibility, more candidly and brutally than almost any other philosopher, that human existence may be pointless in the most squalid and farcical of ways. It is also because much of what he has to say is surely true. On the whole, human history has indeed been more a tale of scarcity, misery, and exploitation than it has been a fable of civility and enlightenment. Those who assume that there must indeed be a meaning to life, and an uplifting one at that, have to confront the cheerless challenge of a Schopenhauer. His work forces them to struggle hard to make their vision seem anything more than anodyne consolation.

---

[17] Ibid. i. 196.

Chapter 3
The eclipse of meaning

Consider this brief exchange in Anton Chekhov's play *Three Sisters*:

> MASHA: Isn't there some meaning?
> TOOZENBACH: Meaning? ... Look out there, it's snowing. What's the meaning of that?

The snow is not a statement or a symbol. It is not, as far as we can tell, an allegory of the fact that the heavens are grieving. It is not trying to say anything, in the way that Philip Larkin imagines spring to be doing:

> The trees are coming into leaf
> Like something almost being said ...
>
> 'The Trees'

Yet to say 'Look out there, it's snowing' already involves quite a few meanings. The snow is 'meaningful' in the sense of being part of an intelligible world, one organized and opened up by our language. It is not just some kind of freakish enigma. It would not be all that odd for someone who had never seen snow before to ask 'What is the meaning of that?' And though the snow is not a symbol of anything, it might well be seen as a signifier. It signifies, perhaps, that winter is coming on. As such, it belongs to a meteorological system powered by laws we can comprehend. This kind of meaning, we may note, is 'inherent' rather than 'ascribed': snow means that winter is coming on whatever we may happen to think it means. The fact that it is snowing can also be *used* as a signifier: in fact, Toozenbach is doing just this, pointing to the snow (ironically enough) as a sign of meaninglessness. Or someone might exclaim 'Look at the snow – winter's coming on! We'd better get started for Moscow', which makes the snow a signifier within a human project, the basis of a message between individuals. In all these senses, snowing is not just snowing.

Perhaps Toozenbach is trying to suggest that the world is absurd. But 'absurdity' is a meaning, too. To cry 'But that's absurd!' evokes some possibility of coherent sense-making. Absurdity makes sense only in contrast to such sense-making, rather as doubting makes sense only against a background of certainty. To someone who claims that life is meaningless, we can always retort: '*What* is it that is meaningless?'; and his response to that has to be couched in terms of meanings. People who ask after the meaning of life are usually asking what all its various situations add up to; and since to identify a situation itself involves meaning, they cannot be lamenting that there is no meaning at all. Just as it is an empty gesture to doubt everything, so it is hard to see how life could be absurd all the way through. It might be pointless all the way through, in the sense of lacking a given end or purpose; but it cannot be absurd in the sense of being nonsensical unless there is some logic by which we can measure this fact.

Perhaps, however, life seems absurd in contrast to a meaning which it used to have, or which you believe it used to have. One reason why modernists like Chekhov are so preoccupied with the possibility of meaninglessness is that modernism is old enough to remember a time when there was still meaning in plenty, or at least so the rumour has it. Meaning was around recently enough for Chekhov, Conrad, Kafka, Beckett, and their colleagues to feel stunned and dispirited by its draining away. The typical modernist work of art is still haunted by the memory of an orderly universe, and so is nostalgic enough to feel the eclipse of meaning as an anguish, a scandal, an intolerable deprivation. This is why such works so often turn around a central absence, some cryptic gap or silence which marks the spot through which sense-making has leaked away. One thinks of Chekhov's Moscow in *Three Sisters*, Conrad's African heart of darkness, Virginia Woolf's blankly enigmatic lighthouse, E. M. Forster's empty Marabar caves, T. S. Eliot's still point of the turning world, the non-encounter at the heart of Joyce's *Ulysses*, Beckett's Godot, or the nameless crime of Kafka's Joseph K. In this tension between the persisting need for meaning and the gnawing sense of its elusiveness, modernism can be genuinely tragic.

Postmodernism, by contrast, is not really old enough to recall a time when there was truth, meaning, and reality, and treats such fond delusions with the brusque impatience of youth. There is no point in pining for depths that never existed. The fact that they seem to have vanished does not mean that life is superficial, since you can only have surfaces if you have depths to contrast with them. The Meaning of meanings is not a firm foundation but an oppressive illusion. To live without the need for such guarantees is to be free. You can argue that there were indeed once grand narratives (Marxism, for example) which corresponded to something real, but that we are well rid of them; or you can insist that these narratives were nothing but a chimera all along, so that there was never anything to be lost. Either the world is no longer story-shaped, or it never was in the first place.

Callow though much postmodernist thought is on this question, there is one point on which it is surely suggestive. The nausea of a Jean-Paul Sartre or the tragic defiance of an Albert Camus, when confronted with a supposedly meaningless world, is really part of the problem to which it is a response. You are only likely to feel that the world is sickeningly pointless, as opposed to just plain old pointless, if you had inflated expectations of it in

the first place. Camus and Sartre are, so to speak, old enough
to recall a time when the world seemed meaningful; but if they
believe that this was an illusion even then, what exactly has
been lost by its disappearance? Life may not have a built-in
purpose, but that is not to say that it is futile. The nihilist is just a
disillusioned metaphysician. *Angst* is just the flip side of faith. It
is the same with renegade Roman Catholics, who tend to become
card-carrying atheists rather than High-Church Anglicans. It
is only because you falsely imagined that the world could be
somehow inherently meaningful – an idea that postmodernism
finds senseless – that you are so devastated to find that it is not.

It is possible to see the work of Samuel Beckett as stranded
somewhere between modernist and postmodernist cases. In his
sense of the extreme elusiveness of meaning (his favourite word,
he once remarked, was 'perhaps'), Beckett is classically modernist.
His writing is woven through from end to end with a sense of its
own provisionality, ironically aware that it might just as well never
have existed. This is why it seems only *just* to exist – to hover
precariously on the edge of articulation, before lapsing listlessly
away into some wordless darkness. It is as thin as is compatible
with being barely perceptible. Meaning flares and fades, erasing
itself almost as soon as it emerges. One pointless narrative cranks
itself laboriously off the ground, only to be aborted in mid-stream
for another, equally futile one. There is not even enough meaning
to be able to give a name to what is awry with us.

Everything in this post-Auschwitz world is ambiguous and
indeterminate. Every proposition is a tentative hypothesis. It is
hard to be sure whether anything is happening or not, for what
in this world would count as an event? Is waiting for Godot an
occurrence, or the suspension of one? The act of waiting is a kind
of nothing, a perpetual deferment of meaning, an anticipation of
the future which is also a way of life in the present. This suggests
that to live is to defer, to put off a final meaning; and though
the act of postponing it makes life hard to bear, it may also be

8. Vladimir and Estragon from Samuel Beckett's play *Waiting for Godot*

what keeps it in motion. How in any case, in a world where sense-making is so frail and fragmentary, would you recognize such a resplendent meaning? Perhaps Vladimir and Estragon in *Waiting for Godot* have already failed to recognize it; maybe Pozzo is in fact Godot (they might have misheard the name) and they do not realize it. Or maybe this whole agonized, farcical freezing of time *is* Godot's coming, as for the philosopher Walter Benjamin the very emptiness of history points by a kind of negation to the imminent arrival of the Messiah. Perhaps Godot's arrival will be a salutary disenchantment, revealing that there was no need for it in the first place – that there was never one big thing that was crying out for redemption, but that this belief is itself part of our false consciousness. This might be akin to Walter Benjamin's vision of a Messiah who will indeed transform the world, but who will do so by making minor adjustments.

If the world is indeterminate, then despair is not possible. An ambiguous reality must surely leave room for hope. Perhaps this is one reason why the tramps (though who says they are tramps?) do not kill themselves. There is no death in Beckett, just an unending process of degeneration – of limbs stiffening up, skin flaking off, eyeballs blurring, and hearing thickening, a decay which seems likely to go on for all eternity. Godot's absence seems to have plunged life into radical indeterminacy, but that means that there is no assurance that he will not come. If everything is indeterminate, then this must be true of our knowledge of it as well, in which case we cannot rule out the possibility that there is a secret plot to it all. Even bleakness cannot be absolute in a world without absolutes. It appears that there can be no salvation in this sort of world, even though it strikes us as the kind of place where the idea of redemption might still make sense; but then there may be no absolute need for it either. Anyway, who is to say that, viewed from some other perspective altogether, this landscape of freaks, cripples, and hairless spheres of flesh is not teetering on the brink of transformation?

It seems, to say the least, highly unlikely. Yet the fact that nothing in Beckett is definitive, that every broken signifier shuttles us on to the next, can be seen not only as an allegory of desire, but as an allegory of meaning. Meaning is also an endlessly unfinished process, a shuffling from one sign to another without fear or hope of closure. We can be sure of one thing at least about any piece of meaning, that there's always more where that came from. There could not logically be a final meaning, one which brought interpretation to a halt, since it would need to be interpreted. And since signs have meaning only in relation to other signs, there could no more be one big final sign than there could be one number, or one person.

In Beckett's world, the fact that there is always more meaning where that came from generally means more suffering. Yet this withdrawal of ultimate meaning is also enabling, since it creates the space in which we can momentarily survive. It is true that to survive and flourish requires more guarantees than are available in Beckett's depleted universe; but guarantees which are too robust tend to stunt our flourishing as well. 'Perhaps' is among other things Beckett's response to the Fascist absolutism against which, as a member of the French Resistance, he fought so courageously. If it is true that we need a degree of certainty to get by, it is also true that too much of the stuff can be lethal. In the meantime, something apparently unkillable keeps taking its course, with all the humdrum, anonymous, implacable quality of a process of digestion.

The evaporation of stable meaning is one reason why it is hard to describe Beckett's work as tragic, since it seems too indeterminate for that. Another reason is its resolute banality, its satirical Irish debunking and deflating. It is a strain of anti-Literature, one which subverts the heady rhetoric of achievement. These are writings which preserve a secret compact with failure, with the fatiguing, unglamorous business of staying biologically afloat. Beckett's scooped-out, amnesiac human figures are not even up to the dignity of being tragic protagonists, which would at least be a stable signification of sorts. They are not even well-organized enough to hang themselves. We are in the presence of low farce or black carnivalesque rather than high drama. As with the Second World War, extremity is simply the order of the day. It seems that we cannot even call our suffering our own, since the human subject has imploded along with the history to which it belongs. To assign a memory or experience to this human subject rather than that one requires a degree of assurance which is no longer easy to come by.

Very little in Beckett's writing is stable or self-identical; and the puzzle is then how things can be at once so inconstant and so persistently painful. Yet the paradox of his work is that it retains its nostalgia for truth and meaning, even though there is a meaning-shaped hole at its centre. The other face of the elusiveness and ambiguity is Beckett's monkish devotion to precision, his Irish scholasticism of mind. What seems eccentric about his writing is its pedantic way with mere wisps and scraps of meaning, its meticulous sculpting of sheer vacancy, its crazedly clear-headed attempt to eff the ineffable. His art takes a set of postulates, and in quasi-structuralist manner lets them run through their various mechanical permutations, until the process is exhausted and another, equally meaningless set of permutations takes over. Complete dramas are conjured out of reshuffled arrangements of the same few scraps and leavings. Beckett's world may be mystifying, but his approach to it is one of cold-eyed demystification. His language pares austerely away at the inessential, shrinking and hacking to the bone. It betrays a Protestant animus against the superfluous and ornamental. Sparseness is perhaps the closest one can come to the truth. The reader is packed off poorer but more honest. What strikes us is the extreme scrupulousness with which his work weaves the wind, the rigorous logic with which it trades in hints and absurdities. Beckett's materials may be raw and random, but his treatment of them is ironically stylized, with a balletic elegance and economy of gesture. It is as though the whole formal apparatus of truth, logic, and reason remains intact, even though its contents have leaked away.

The other side of Beckett's work, however, is a kind of postmodern positivism, for which things are not endlessly elusive but brutely themselves. As his Parisian contemporary Jean-Paul Sartre writes in *Being and Nothingness*: 'Uncreated, without reason for being, without any connection with another being, being-in-itself is superfluous for all eternity.'[18] This reflects the side of Beckett for which the world just is whatever is the case, the artist who is fascinated by the sheer inert materiality of objects like pebbles or bowler hats, and who resists the attempt to impose on them some portentous significance ('No symbol where none intended', as he writes). Chief among these inert objects, though with no particular privileged status, is the body, on which meaning never seems to stick. The body is simply a lumbering mechanism, which we perch inside as a man might sit inside a crane. Things in Beckett's world are either so low-profiled as to be desperately ambiguous, or bluntly impervious to meaning. Reality is either a rock face which offers no hold for sense-making, or an enigmatic flickering of signifiers. It is shadowy and evanescent, but also a place of sharp edges and heavy weights, of crushing physical pains and splintering bones.

On this second, 'postmodern' way of looking, life is not meaningful, but neither is it meaningless. To claim gloomily that existence is bereft of meaning is to remain a prisoner of the illusion that it might have meaning. But what if life is just not the kind of thing which can be spoken of in either of these terms? If meaning is something people do, how can we expect the world to be meaningful or meaningless in itself? And why then should we bewail the fact that it does not present itself to us as bursting

[18] Jean-Paul Sartre, *Being and Nothingness* (London, 1958), p. xlii (translation amended).

with significance? You would not lament the fact that you were not born wearing a small woolly hat. Babies being born sporting small woolly hats is just not the kind of thing one should expect to happen. There is no point in feeling down in the mouth about it. It is no cause for tragic *Angst* that you came into the world bareheaded. It is not a lack which you are glumly aware of as you go about your daily business.

Nothing is missing here, just as nothing is missing when I reply 'Because I put it on the gas' when asked 'Why is the kettle boiling?' Someone, however, might suspect that I have not really explained why the kettle is boiling unless I also explain the chemical processes which underlie this, and then the laws which underlie that, and so on until we have reached a bedrock where all questions come to an end. Unless there is an absolute foundation, there must surely be something lacking. Everything must be left hanging precariously in the air. And this, for some people, is the case with meaning. Surely, if meaning is simply something we get up to, it cannot act as a sure infrastructure to reality. Things must be inherently meaningful, not just meaningful because we make them so. And all these meanings must add up to one overall one. Unless there is a Meaning of meanings, there is no meaning at all. If the fact that it is snowing does not signify that God is seeking to shroud the earth in a soft mantle of oblivion, then it must simply be absurd.

What is an 'inherent' meaning in any case? For meanings are not 'in' things in the sense that ink is in a bottle. There could be a significant design somewhere in the world without our knowing about it (an unseen snowflake, for example, or an as-yet undetected sociological pattern); but meanings in the more common senses of the word are surely not like this. They are interpretations of the world, and therefore dependent upon us. Talk of 'inherent' meanings comes down to talk about trying to describe what is actually there in reality. But it is we who do the describing. We can then contrast this with 'assigned' meanings such as 'Greenland'. There are also obviously subjective meanings, such as 'For me, the Chicago skyline is the profile of God', or 'Whenever I hear the word "pelvis" I always think of Abraham Lincoln'.

We shall see later that we can talk of meanings as somehow built into things, or as the kind of natures they have. For the most part, however, 'inherent' meanings are simply the bits of our language which get at what is there. And sometimes there are situations, such as whatever it was that happened to the *Mary Celeste*, in which we simply do not know what is there, and where the truth may be quite other than all of our current interpretations. How does this affect the debate over the meaning of life? It is possible that life could have an 'inherent' meaning in the sense of one which none of us knows anything about – one quite different from the various meanings we fashion from it in our individual lives. Sigmund Freud, for example, came to believe that the meaning of life was death – that the whole effort of *Eros* or the life-instincts was to return to a condition of death-like stasis, where the ego could no longer be harmed. If this is true (and of course it may not be), then it follows that it was true before Freud discovered the fact, and that it is true right now even for those who do not recognize it. Our drives and desires may form a pattern of which we are unconscious, yet which fundamentally determines the meaning of our existence. There may thus be a meaning to life which we are (or were) all entirely ignorant of, yet which was not put there by some supra-human force like God or the *Zeitgeist*. To put the point a little more technically: immanence does not necessarily imply transcendence. A meaning to life put there by God, and one conjured up by ourselves, may not be the only possibilities.

As far as the apparent conflict between 'ascribed' and 'inherent' meanings goes, take the business of language. There used to be a debate in literary criticism about whether the meaning of a poem is somehow already there in the work, waiting for the reader to come and pluck it out, or whether it is something that we, the readers, bring to the poem. If it is we who invest the poem with meaning, then don't we simply get out of it whatever we put into it? In that case, how could the poem ever surprise us, or make us feel that it is resisting the way we are trying to read it? There is an analogy here with the idea that life is what you make it. Does this mean that we only get out of life what we put into it? 'Ultimately', writes Nietzsche, 'man finds in things nothing but what he himself has imported into them.'[19] So if you find that your life is empty, why not just fill it, as you would fill the fridge when you have run out of food? Why wail loudly about the fact when the solution is so obviously at hand? This theory of meaning, however, seems troublingly narcissistic. Do we never get outside our own heads? Isn't a genuine meaning one which we feel ourselves running up against, one which can resist or rebuff us, one which bears in on us with a certain ineluctability? If life is to have a meaning, surely it cannot be whatever we whimsically project on to it. Surely life itself must have a say in the matter?

We shall be looking at how life might resist what we try to make of it in a moment. Meanwhile, we can examine more closely the idea of meaning being 'in' a poem. To say that in the phrase 'Shall I compare thee to a summer's day?', the meaning lies 'in' the words themselves is just to say that the words have an agreed meaning in the English language. This is an agreement which cuts far deeper than whatever *I* might want the words to mean, and which is ultimately bound up with sharing a practical form of life. The fact that there is agreement here does not mean that we cannot argue over what these words mean in this particular context. Perhaps 'Shall I?' here means 'Do you want me to?', or perhaps it means 'Is it true that in the future I will compare you to a summer's day?' It is just that what we are arguing over are not meanings that we ascribe arbitrarily to the words. Even so, these meanings are only 'in' the words because of the social conventions which determine

---

[19] Nietzsche, *Will to Power*, 327.

the fact that in English the letters *d-a-y* should stand for the time between sunrise and sunset, the letters *t-h-e-e* should be the accusative case of the old-fashioned personal pronoun 'thou', and so on. These conventions are certainly arbitrary when viewed from the outside, as a comparison with the words for 'day' and 'thee' in Bulgarian would make clear. But they are not arbitrary when seen from the inside, any more than the rules of chess are.

To say that meaning is 'inherent' – that it is somehow built into things or situations themselves, rather than foisted on them – may be a misleading way of talking; but it is possible, even so, to make some sense of it. Some objects, for example, could be said to express or embody meanings in their very material presence. The paradigmatic case of this is a work of art. What is strange about works of art is that they seem material and meaningful at the same time. At the start of this book, I touched on the case that objects like cardiographs cannot be meaningful in themselves because meaning is a matter of language, not of things. But because a cardiograph, unlike a cabbage, is a human artefact, it can surely be said to have meanings and intentions built into it. It has, after all, a specific function in the world of medicine, which is independent of whatever functions I might choose to assign it. I can always use it to wedge open the window on a stifling hot day, or wield it with enviable dexterity to fight off a homicidal maniac; but it is still a cardiograph I am using to do so.

For those who believe in God, or some other intelligent force behind the universe, life has built-in meanings and purposes because it is itself an artefact. It is, to be sure, an appallingly shoddy piece of work in many ways, apparently thrown off in one of the artist's less inspired moments. But you can speak of inherent meaning here, just as you can with an armchair. To say that an armchair is 'intentional' is not to suggest that it harbours secret wishes, but that it is structured for the purpose of achieving certain effects, namely having people sit in it. This is a meaning or function it has independently of what I might want it to mean.

But it is not a meaning independent of humanity altogether. It is structured this way because someone designed it this way.

When we wonder whether a particular situation is, say, an instance of racism, we are asking about the situation itself, not just about how we feel about it or the language we use to describe it. Seeing meanings such as 'prejudiced' and 'discriminatory' as 'inherent' in the situation is just a pretentious way of saying that the situation really is racist. If we do not see this – if we think, for example, that 'racism' is just a set of subjective meanings we impose on the bare facts of what is happening – then we are not seeing the situation for what it is. A description of it which lacked such terms as 'discriminatory' – which tried, for example, to be 'value-free' – would not adequately capture what was going on. It would fail as a description, not just as an evaluation. This does not necessarily mean that the meaning of the situation is blindingly obvious. Whether it is racist or not may turn out to be impossible to determine. This, no doubt, is what people mean when they claim that it is possible to 'construct' the situation in conflicting ways. Words like 'racism' embody arguable interpretations. But it is the truth of the situation we are talking about, not the meaning of our interpretations.

Let us put the issue the other way round. Let us ask not what an 'inherent' meaning might look like, but what it means to claim that meanings are what we 'construct' the world to be. Does this imply that we can 'construct' it any old way we like? Surely not. Nobody actually believes this, not least because everybody agrees that our interpretations can sometimes be mistaken. It is just that the reasons people give for why this is so tend to differ. All of them, however, agree that it just would not *work* for us to 'construct' tigers as coy and cuddly. For one thing, some of us would no longer be around to tell the tale. Some thinkers would point out that it simply would not fit in with the rest of our interpretations, whereas others would argue that this perception of tigers would not allow us to do agreeable, life-enhancing things such as running away from them as fast as we can when they flash their fangs. Other theorists, known as realists, would argue that we cannot see tigers as cuddly because it is not the case that tigers are cuddly. How do we know? Because we have strong evidence that they are not, which comes to us from a world that is independent of our interpretations of it.

Whatever one's position here, it seems true that the distinction between 'inherent' and 'ascribed' is useful enough for some purposes, but in other ways is ripe for dismantling. For one thing, quite a few so-called inherent meanings, like pagan notions of Destiny, the Christian pattern of redemption, or Hegel's Idea, involve people making sense of their own lives. On this view, men and women are not just the puppets of some grandiose Truth, as they are for Schopenhauer. There *is* such a Truth in these cases; but without men and women's active participation in it, it will not unfold. It is part of Oedipus's tragic fate that he actively, if blindly, helps to bring on his own catastrophe. For Christian faith, the kingdom of God will not arrive unless human beings co-operate in its creation, even though the fact that they do this is already reckoned into the very idea of the kingdom. For Hegel, Reason realizes itself in history only through the genuinely free actions of individuals; indeed, it is at its most real when they are at their most free. All of these grand narratives dismantle the distinction between freedom and necessity – between forging your own meanings and being receptive to one already installed in the world.

All meanings are human performances, and 'inherent' meanings are just those performances which manage to capture something of the truth of the matter. The world does not divide down the middle between those who believe that meanings are 'inherent' in things in the same sense that my appendix is buried in my abdomen, and those rather weird people for whom the idea of 'having an appendix' is just a 'social construction' of the human body. (For sound medical reasons, not all of these people are around to tell the tale either.) 'Constructions' of this kind are a kind of one-way conversation with the world, in which, rather like the Americans in Iraq, it is we who tell it what it is like. But meaning is in fact the product of a transaction between us and reality. Texts and readers are mutually dependent.

To revert to our question-and-answer model: We can pose questions to the world, and these are certainly our questions rather than its own. But the answers the world may return are instructive precisely because reality is always more than our questioning anticipates. It exceeds our own interpretations of it, and is not averse to greeting them from time to time with a rude gesture or knocking the stuffing out of them. Meaning, to be sure, is something people do; but they do it in dialogue with a determinate world whose laws they did not invent, and if their meanings are to be valid, they must respect this world's grain and texture. To recognize this is to cultivate a certain humility, one which is at odds with the 'constructivist' axiom that when it comes to meaning, it is we who are all-important. This superficially radical notion is in fact secretly in cahoots with a Western ideology for which what matters is the meanings we stamp on the world and others for our own ends.

Shakespeare was alive to these issues, as this exchange in *Troilus and Cressida* over the worth of Helen of Troy makes clear:

> TROILUS: What's aught but as 'tis valued?
> HECTOR: But value dwells not in particular will:
> It holds his estimate and dignity
> As well wherein 'tis precious of itself
> As in the prizer...

> Act 2, scene 2

Troilus is a kind of existentialist for whom things are valueless and meaningless in themselves; they acquire value and meaning only through the human energies which are invested in them.

In his eyes, Helen is precious because she has been the cause of a glorious war, rather than having caused a war because she is precious. The less hot-headed Hector, by contrast, holds to a more 'intrinsicist' theory of value: in his eyes, value is an amalgam of the given and the created. Things are not just highly prized, but precious or worthless in themselves. To some extent, he is surely right: health, peace, justice, love, happiness, humour, mercy, and so on are all candidates for the category of the inherently valuable. So are things like food, water, warmth, and shelter, which we need for our survival. But a lot that Hector himself probably thinks inherently valuable – gold, let's say – is actually valuable only by common agreement. Shakespeare is well aware of the parallels between value and meaning. His plays brood constantly on the question of whether meanings are innate or relative. He lived, after all, at a point of historical transition from a faith in the former to a belief in the latter; and his drama relates this momentous shift to an economic shift from 'intrinsic' values to the 'exchange-values' generated by market forces.[20]

The quarrel between 'inherentists' and 'constructivists' runs back well beyond the Elizabethan age. In an illuminating study, Frank Farrell traces it as far back as the late medieval period, and the conflict between Catholic and Protestant theologies.[21] The problem is that if God is to be all-powerful, the world cannot be allowed to have inherent or essential meanings, since these would inevitably constrain his freedom of action. Creation cannot be permitted to put up resistance to its Creator. It cannot have a mind and autonomy of its own. So the only way to preserve God's freedom and omnipotence seemed to be to drain the world of inherent sense. Reality for some Protestant thinkers had accordingly to be thinned out, stripped of the thickness which Catholic theologians like Thomas Aquinas ascribed to it. It had

---

[20] For a fuller discussion, see my *William Shakespeare* (Oxford, 1986).
[21] See Frank Farrell, *Subjectivity, Realism and Postmodernism* (Cambridge, 1996).

to be radically indeterminate, for then it would just be pliable stuff which the Almighty could bend into whatever shape he whimsically chose. He would no longer have to respect the fact that, say, a woman is a woman, since he could quite easily make her behave like a hedgehog if the idea took his fancy. The world, as with postmodernism, becomes one enormous cosmetic surgery.

Essences – the idea that things, including human beings, had determinate natures – thus had to go. If they lingered on, they would get in the way of God's supreme power. The 'realists' who believed in such determinate natures were at daggers drawn with the 'nominalists' who saw them simply as verbal fictions. Protestantism of this kind is thus an early form of anti-essentialism. As with some anti-essentialism today, it goes hand in hand with a kind of voluntarism, or cult of the will. Once determinate natures have disappeared, God's arbitrary will can finally come into its own. Things will then be what they are because of his say-so, not because of themselves. Postmodernism simply replaces God here with human beings. Reality is not any way in itself, just the way that we construct it to be.

For the voluntarist, torture is morally wrong because God's will has determined it to be so, not because it is wrong in itself. In fact, nothing is right or wrong in itself. God could easily have decided to make failing to torture each other a punishable offence. There can be no reason for his decisions, since reasons would hamper his absolute freedom of action. Anti-essentialism thus goes hand in hand with irrationalism. Like all tyrants, God is an anarchist, unbound by law or reason. He is the source of his own law and reason, which are there to serve his power. Torture could well be permissible if it suited his purposes. It is not difficult to identify the inheritors of these doctrines in our own political world.

Yet purging the world of essences may not clear the decks for the unbridled will. For what if in clearing out essences, you find you have swept out the self along with them? If the self has no determinate nature either, then its will and agency are fatally undermined. At the point of its supreme triumph, it is struck empty. The news that there is no given meaning to life is both exhilarating and alarming. The individual self has now taken over God's role as a supreme legislator; yet, like God, it seems to be legislating in a void. Its diktats appear every bit as arbitrary and pointless as divine commands. In moral matters, this sometimes takes the form of what is known as 'decisionism': infanticide is wrong because I, or we, have taken some fundamental moral decision from which such prohibitions follow. As Nietzsche remarks: 'Genuine philosophers... are commanders and legislators: they say: *thus* shall it be!'[22] At once solitary and triumphant, the self is now the only source of meaning and value in a world bleached of inherent significance. Yet this meaninglessness seems also to have invaded its own inner sanctum. Like the Almighty, it is free to inscribe its own meanings on the blank slate of the cosmos; yet since there is now no objective reason why it should act in this way rather than that, this freedom turns out to be vacuous and self-consuming. Humanity itself has become an absurdity.

The Protestant self is no longer at home in the world. There are no longer any given bonds between the two. Because reality is inherently meaningless, the self can find no reflection of itself in reality, which is made out of a material utterly different from its own. It is thus not long before it comes like a castaway to doubt its own existence, deprived of anything outside itself which might confirm its identity. 'Man' is the sole source of meaning in the world; but the world has turned its back on such sense-making, thus rendering it arbitrary and gratuitous. And because there is no sense or logic in things, there is no predictability in them either. This is why the Protestant self moves fearfully in a darkened world

---

[22] Friedrich Nietzsche, *Beyond Good and Evil*, in Walter Kaufmann (ed.), *Basic Writings of Nietzsche* (New York, 1968), 326.

of random forces, haunted by a hidden God, uncertain of its own salvation.

All this, to be sure, was at the same time an enormous liberation. There was no longer simply one valid way of reading reality. The priests no longer monopolized the keys to the kingdom of meaning. Freedom of interpretation was now possible. Men and women no longer had to kowtow to the ready-made meanings which God had folded into the world. The sacred text of the universe, in which physical elements were allegorical signs of spiritual truths, gradually gave way to a secular script. Emptied of prefabricated meanings, reality could now be construed according to the needs and desires of humanity. What were previously fixed meanings could be loosened up and combined in imaginative new ways. Significantly, it was a Protestant pastor, Friedrich Schleiermacher, who invented the science of hermeneutics, or interpretation. It is even arguable that this whole way of seeing has sound scriptural roots. In Genesis 2: 19, 'the Lord God formed every beast of the field and every bird of the air, and brought them to the man to see what he would call them; and whatever the man called every living creature, that was its name' (RSV). Since the act of naming in ancient Judaic culture is always a creative or performative one, this suggests that it is humanity which is the source of meaning, while Yahweh is the source of being. God makes the animals, presents them to man, and they become what he makes of them.

Should the lonely Protestant spirit groping fearfully in the dark be a cause for concern for those who believe that life is what you make it? Yes and no. No, in the sense that making your life meaningful, rather than expecting its meaning to be pre-given, is a perfectly plausible idea. Yes, in so far as it ought to serve as a sober warning that to shape the meaning of one's life for oneself cannot be a matter of fashioning just any meaning that takes your fancy. It does not exempt you from justifying whatever it is that makes your life meaningful at the bar of common opinion. You cannot just say 'Personally, I find that the meaning of my life lies in asphyxiating dormice' and hope to get away with it.

Nor can it be a question of creation *ex nihilo*. Human beings are self-determining – but only on the basis of a deeper dependency upon Nature, the world, and each other. And whatever meaning I may forge for my own life is constrained from the inside by this dependency. We cannot start from scratch. It is not a matter of clearing away God-given meanings in order to hammer out our own, as Nietzsche seemed to imagine. For we are already plunged deep in the midst of meaning, wherever it is we happen to find ourselves. We are woven through by the meanings of others – meanings which we never got to choose, yet which provide the matrix within which we come to make sense of ourselves and the world. In this sense, if not in every sense, the idea that I can determine the meaning of my own life is an illusion.

But it is not only what others make of their lives which restricts what I can make of my own. It is also shaped by those features of my existence which arise from my being a member of a natural species, and which are most obvious in the material nature of my body. It could not be part of the meaning of life that I should leap unaided thirty feet in the air three times a day. Any meaningful life-plan which fails to accommodate the realities of kinship, sociality, sexuality, death, play, mourning, laughter, sickness, labour, communication, and so on is not going to get us very far. It is true that these universal aspects of human life are lived out very differently by different cultures; but it is also worth noting that they bulk large in the course of any individual existence. Many of the central features of personal life are not personal at all. Simply because we are material animals, an enormous amount has already been determined for us, not least the ways in which we come to reason. For our style of reasoning is closely connected to our animality.[23] Perhaps this is part of what Wittgenstein had in mind when he remarked that if a lion could speak, we would not be able to understand what he said. Unless the meaning of life encompasses my material body and my membership of the species, it cannot be said to encompass me. We shall unpack some of the implications of this in the next chapter.

---

[23] See Alasdair MacIntyre, *Dependent Rational Animals* (London, 1998).

Chapter 4
Is life what you make it?

So far, we have looked more at meaning than at life. Yet the word 'life' is every bit as problematic as the word 'meaning', and it is not hard to see why. For surely the reason why we cannot talk about the meaning of life is that there is no such thing as life? Are we not, as Wittgenstein might say, bewitched here by our grammar, which can generate the word 'life' in the singular just as it can the word 'tomato'? Perhaps we have the word 'life' only because our language is intrinsically reifying. '*Essence* is expressed by grammar', as Wittgenstein remarks.[24] How on earth could everything that falls under the heading of human life, from childbirth to clog dancing, be thought to stack up to a single meaning? Isn't this exactly the delusion of the paranoiac, for whom everything is supposed to be ominously resonant of everything else, bound together in an oppressively translucent whole? Or, if you prefer, the delusion of philosophy, which as Freud mischievously commented is the nearest thing to paranoia? Not even an individual life adds up to a unified whole. It is true that some people see their lives as forming an elegant narrative all the way from Introduction to Epilogue, but not everyone views themselves like this. How, then, could countless millions of individual lives stack up to a coherent whole, if not even one of

---

[24] Ludwig Wittgenstein, *Philosophical Investigations*, trans. G. E. M. Anscombe (Oxford, 1963), §371.

them does? Life surely does not have enough shape to it even to constitute a riddle.

'The meaning of life' might well mean 'what it all adds up to', in which case childbirth and clog dancing would indeed have to be viewed as aspects of a single, significant totality. And this is more than one would expect even from the most shapely, well-integrated works of art. Not even the most grandiose of historical narratives imagines that it can make sense of absolutely everything. Marxism has nothing to say about the anal scent glands of the civet, a silence which it does not consider a defect. There is no official Buddhist position on West Yorkshire waterfalls. It is wildly improbable that everything in human life constitutes part of a coherent pattern. Is it enough, then, for most of it to do so? Or does 'the meaning of life' mean rather 'the *essential* significance of life' – not so much what it all adds up to as what it all boils down to? A statement like 'The meaning of life is suffering' suggests not that suffering is the whole of life, or the point and purpose of life, but that it is the most significant or fundamental feature of it. By tracking this particular thread, so the claim goes, we can make sense of the whole baffling design.

Is there, then, a phenomenon called 'human life' which can be the bearer of a coherent meaning? Well, people certainly sometimes speak of life in such general terms. Life is a gas, a bitch, a cabaret, a vale of tears, a bed of roses. This bunch of shop-soiled tags may hardly seem much on which to build a case. Yet the assumption that all meta-statements about human life are vacuous is itself vacuous. It is not true that only concrete, particular truths have any force. What, for example, of the generalization that most men and women in history have lived lives of fruitless, wretched toil? This is surely more disturbing than the proposition that most people in Delaware have done so.

Perhaps it is impossible to generalize intelligently about human life, because in order to do so we would have to step outside it.

And this would be like trying to leap out of our skins. Surely only someone outside human existence altogether, like God, would be able to survey it as a whole and see whether it added up?[25] The case is akin to Nietzsche's argument in *The Twilight of the Idols* that life cannot be judged either valuable or valueless in itself, since the criteria we would have to appeal to in order to establish this would themselves be part of life. But this is surely questionable. You do not need to stand outside human existence in order to make meaningful comments about it, any more than you need to be in New Zealand in order to criticize British society as a whole. It is true that nobody has ever actually seen British society as a whole, any more than anyone has ever clapped eyes on the Boy Scout movement; but we can make reasonable inferences from the bits of reality that we are familiar with to the bits that we aren't. It is not a matter of seeing it all, just a matter of seeing enough to sort out what seems typical from what does not.

If generalizations about humanity can be valid, it is among other things because human beings, belonging as they do to the same natural species, share an immense amount in common. To say this is not to overlook the politically explosive differences and distinctions between them. But those postmodern thinkers who are enraptured by difference, and with dreary uniformity find it everywhere they turn, should not overlook our common features either. The differences between human beings are vital, but they are not a solid enough foundation on which to build an ethics or a politics.

Besides, even if one could not speak of 'the human condition' in 1500, one can certainly do so in 2000. Those who find the idea objectionable seem not to have heard of globalization. It is

[25] John Cottingham seems to endorse this case in his *On the Meaning of Life* (London, 2003), and adduces Wittgenstein's *Tractatus Logico-Philosophicus* in its defence. For the Wittgenstein of the *Tractatus*, however, it is not only the meaning of life which falls beyond the bounds of the knowable, but subjectivity as such.

transnational capitalism which has helped to forge humanity into one. What we now at least have in common is the will to survive in the face of the various threats to our existence which loom up on every side. There is a sense in which those who deny the reality of the human condition also deny global warming. Nothing ought to unite the species as effectively as the possibility of its extinction. In death, at least, we come together.

If the meaning of life lies in the common *goal* of human beings, then there seems no doubt about what this is. What everyone strives for is happiness. 'Happiness', to be sure, is a feeble, holiday-camp sort of word, evocative of manic grins and cavorting about in a multicoloured jacket. But as Aristotle recognizes in his *Nicomachean Ethics*, it operates as a kind of baseline in human life, in the sense that you cannot reasonably ask *why* we should seek to be happy. It is not a means to something else, as money or power generally are. It is more like wanting to be respected. Desiring it just seems to be part of our nature. Here, then, is a foundational term of sorts. The problem is that it is so desperately indeterminate. The idea of happiness seems both vital and vacuous. What counts as happiness? What if you find it in terrorizing old ladies? Someone who is determined to become an actor may spend fruitless hours auditioning while living on a pittance. For much of the time she is anxious, dispirited, and mildly hungry. She is not what we would usually call happy. Her life is not pleasant or enjoyable. Yet she is, so to speak, prepared to sacrifice her happiness to her happiness.

Happiness is sometimes seen as a state of mind. But this is not how Aristotle regards it. 'Well-being', as we usually translate his term for happiness, is what we might call a state of soul, which for him involves not just an interior condition of being, but a disposition to behave in certain ways. As Ludwig Wittgenstein once remarked, the best image of the soul is the body. If you want to observe someone's 'spirit', look at what they do. Happiness for Aristotle is attained by virtue, and virtue is above all a social

9. A statue of the Greek philosopher Aristotle

practice rather than an attitude of mind. Happiness is part of a practical way of life, not some private inner contentment. On this theory, you could look at someone's conduct over a period of time and exclaim 'He's happy!', as you could not on a more dualistic model of human beings. And he would not have to be beaming or cavorting about either.

Julian Baggini, in his discussion of happiness in *What's It All About?*, fails fully to register this point. In order to illustrate that happiness is not the be-all and end-all of life, he argues that if you are just about to embark on your quest for happiness and see someone sinking in quicksand, it would surely be better to save them than to pursue your own contentment.[26] The language of 'embark on your quest for happiness' is surely telling: for one thing, it makes happiness sound like a private pursuit, and for another thing it makes it sound like a good night out on the town. Indeed, it risks making happiness sound more like pleasure: saving someone from quicksand couldn't be part of it, since it clearly isn't pleasant. In fact, Baggini, in common with most moral philosophers, recognizes elsewhere in his book that pleasure is a passing sensation, while happiness at its best is an enduring condition of being. You can experience intense pleasure without being in the least happy; and just as it seems that you can be happy for dubious reasons (such as terrorizing old ladies), you can also relish morally disreputable pleasures, like rejoicing in your enemy's discomfort.

One objection to Baggini's example is thus surely obvious. Couldn't rescuing someone from quicksand be *part* of one's happiness, rather than a dutiful distraction from it? This is only unclear if one is thinking of happiness along the lines of pleasure, rather than of Aristotelian well-being. For Aristotle, happiness is bound up with the practice of virtue; and though he has nothing in particular to say about rescuing people from quicksand, this

---

[26] Julian Baggini, *What's It All About?* (London, 2004), 97.

would certainly count for his great Christian successor Thomas Aquinas as a sign of well-being. For Aquinas, it would be an example of love, which in his view is not ultimately in conflict with happiness. This is not to say that in Aristotle's eyes happiness and pleasure are simple opposites. On the contrary, virtuous people for him are those who reap pleasure from doing good, and those who do the decent thing without enjoying it are not in his view truly virtuous. But pleasure of a merely bovine or dissolute despot variety is certainly to be contrasted unfavourably with happiness.

Baggini's rather un-Aristotelian idea of happiness is also evident in a scenario he takes from the philosopher Robert Nozick. Suppose that you were plugged into a machine, one rather like the supercomputer in the film *The Matrix*, which allowed you a virtual experience of complete, uninterrupted happiness. Wouldn't most people reject this seductive bliss on account of its unreality? Don't we want to live our lives truthfully, without deception, aware of ourselves as the authors of our own lives, conscious that it is our own strivings and not some manufactured contraption which is responsible for our sense of fulfilment? Baggini believes that most people would indeed reject the happiness machine on these grounds, and he is surely right. But the idea of happiness he offers us here is once again un-Aristotelian. It is a mood or state of consciousness rather than a way of life. It is, in fact, exactly the kind of modern concept of happiness which Aristotle might well have found unintelligible, or at least objectionable. For him, you could not be happy sitting in a machine all your life – not just because your experience would be a matter of simulation rather than reality, but because well-being involves a practical, social form of life. Happiness for Aristotle is not an inward disposition that might then issue in certain actions, but a way of acting which creates certain dispositions.

In Aristotle's eyes, the reason why you could not be really happy sitting in a machine all your life is much the same reason as why you could not be fully happy confined to a wheelchair or an iron lung. It is not, of course, that the disabled cannot know a precious sense of self-fulfilment, just like anyone else; it is simply that to be disabled is to be stymied in one's ability to realize certain powers and capacities. And such realization, on Aristotle's own rather specialist definition, is part of one's happiness or well-being. There are other senses of 'happy' in which disabled people can be perfectly so. Even so, the current mealy-mouthed fashion of denying that the disabled really are disabled, a self-deception especially prominent in a United States for which frailty is an embarrassment and nothing short of success will do, is as much a form of moral hypocrisy as the Victorian habit of denying that the poor were quite likely to be miserable. It belongs with a general Western disavowal of uncomfortable truths, an urge to sweep suffering under the carpet.

Sacrificing one's happiness for the sake of someone else is probably the most morally admirable action one can imagine. But it does not therefore follow that it is the most typical or even the most desirable kind of loving. It is not the most desirable because it is a pity that it is necessary in the first place; and it is not the most typical because, as I shall be arguing in a moment, love at its most typical involves the fullest possible reciprocity. One may love one's small infants to the point of being cheerfully prepared to die for them; but because loving in the fullest sense is something the infants themselves are going to have to learn, the love between you and them cannot be the prototype of human love, any more than can a less precious relationship like one's affection for a loyal old butler. In both cases, the relationship is not equal enough.

Happiness or well-being for Aristotle, then, involves a creative realization of one's typically human faculties. It is as much something you do as something you are. And it cannot be done in isolation, which is one way in which it differs from the pursuit of pleasure. The Aristotelian virtues are for the most part social ones. The idea of self-realization can have something of a virile, red-faced feel to it, as though we are speaking of a kind of spiritual gymnastics. In fact, Aristotle's 'great-souled' moral prototype is much like this: a prosperous Athenian gentleman who is a stranger to failure, loss, and tragedy – interestingly, for the author of one of the world's great treatises on the latter topic. The good man for Aristotle often sounds more like Bill Gates than St Francis of Assisi. It is true that he is concerned not with being successful as this or that kind of person – a businessman, for example, or a politician – but with being successful at being human. For Aristotle, being human is something we have to get good at, and virtuous people are virtuosi of living. Even so, there is something amiss with a theory of happiness for which the idea of a happy woman might well be a contradiction in terms. So would the idea of a happy failure.

For Karl Marx, however, a moral philosopher in Aristotle's lineage, self-realization would also encompass, say, listening to a string quartet, or savouring a peach. Perhaps 'self-fulfilment' has a less strenuous ring to it than 'self-realization'. Happiness is a question of self-fulfilment, which is not to be confused with the Boy Scout or Duke of Edinburgh ideology of seeing life as a series of hurdles to be leapt over and achievements to be stashed beneath the belt. Achievements make sense within the qualitative context of a whole life, not (as in the mountaineering ideology of life) as isolated peaks of attainment.

By and large, people either feel good or they do not, and are generally aware of the fact. One cannot, to be sure, dismiss the influence of so-called false consciousness here. A slave may be conned into believing that he is blissfully content when his behaviour betrays the fact that he is not. We have remarkable resources for rationalizing our wretchedness. But when, for example, an astonishing 92 per cent of the Irish tell pollsters that they are happy, there is not much one can do but believe them. It is true that the Irish have a tradition of geniality to strangers, so perhaps they are claiming to be happy simply to make the pollsters feel happy. But there is no real reason not to take them at their word. In the case of practical or Aristotelian happiness, however, the dangers of self-deception are more acute. For how are you to know that you are living your life virtuously? Perhaps a friend or observer might be a more reliable judge here than you are yourself. In fact, Aristotle might have written his books on ethics partly to put people right about what really counted as happiness. He may have assumed that there was a good deal of false consciousness on the issue. Otherwise it is hard to know why he should recommend a goal which all men and women pursue in any case.

If happiness is a state of mind, then it is arguably dependent on one's material circumstances. It is possible to claim that you can be happy despite those circumstances, a case not far from that of Spinoza or the ancient Stoics. Yet it is grossly improbable that you could feel content living in an unsanitary, overcrowded refugee camp, having just lost your children in some natural disaster. On an Aristotelian view of happiness, however, this is even more obvious. You cannot be brave, honourable, and generous unless you are a reasonably free agent living in the kind of political conditions which foster these virtues. This is why Aristotle sees ethics and politics as intimately bound together. The good life requires a particular kind of political state – in his view, one well supplied with slaves and subjected women, who do the donkey-work while you yourself sally forth to pursue the life of excellence. Happiness or well-being is an institutional affair: it demands the kind of social and political conditions in which you are free to exercise your creative powers. This is less evident when one thinks of happiness, as the liberal tends to do, primarily as an internal or individual affair. Happiness as a state of mind may require untroubled surroundings, but it does not require a particular kind of politics.

Happiness, then, may constitute the meaning of life, but it is not an open-and-shut case. We have seen, for example, that someone may claim to derive happiness from behaving despicably. They may even claim perversely to derive it from unhappiness, as in 'He's never happier than when he's grousing'. There is always, in other words, the problem of masochism. As far as despicable behaviour goes, someone's life may be formally meaningful – meaningful in the sense of being orderly, coherent, exquisitely well-patterned, and full of well-defined goals – while being trivial or even squalid in its moral content. The two may even be interrelated, as in the shrivel-hearted bureaucrat syndrome. There are also, of course, other candidates for the meaning of life apart from happiness: power, love, honour, truth, pleasure, freedom, reason, autonomy, the state, the nation, God, self-sacrifice, contemplation, living according to Nature, the greatest happiness of the greatest number, self-abnegation, death, desire, worldly success, the esteem of one's fellows, reaping as many intense experiences as possible, having a good laugh, and so on. For most people, in practice if not always in theory, life is made meaningful by their relationships with those closest to them, such as partners and children.

A number of these candidates will seem to many people either too trivial, or too instrumental, to count as the meaning of life. Power and wealth belong fairly obviously to the instrumental category; and anything which is instrumental cannot have the fundamental quality which the meaning of life seems to demand, since it exists for the sake of something more fundamental than itself. This is not necessarily to equate the instrumental with the inferior: freedom, at least in some definitions of it, is instrumental, yet most people agree on its preciousness.

It seems doubtful, then, that power can be the meaning of life. All the same, it is a precious human resource, as the powerless are well aware. As with wealth, only those well furnished with it can afford to disdain it. Everything depends on who is exercising it for what purposes in which situations. But it would seem no more an end in itself than wealth – unless, that is, you take 'power' in the Nietzschean sense, which is closer to the idea of self-realization than it is to domination. (Not that Nietzsche was in the least averse to a stiff dose of the latter.) 'Will to power' in Nietzsche's thought means the tendency of all things to realize, expand, and augment themselves; and it is reasonable to see this as an end in itself, just as Aristotle regards human flourishing as an end in itself. Spinoza viewed power in much the same way. It is just that, in Nietzsche's Social Darwinist vision of life, this ceaseless proliferation of powers also involves power as domination, as each life-form strives to subjugate the others. Those tempted to see power in the sense of domination as an end in itself should summon to mind the monstrous, grotesque figure of the deceased British newspaper proprietor Robert Maxwell, a swindler and bully whose body was an obscene image of his soul.

As for wealth, we live in a civilization which piously denies that it is an end in itself, and treats it exactly this way in practice. One of the most powerful indictments of capitalism is that it compels us to invest most of our creative energies in matters which are in fact purely utilitarian. The means of life become the end. Life consists in laying the material infrastructure for living. It is astonishing that in the twenty-first century, the material organization of life should bulk as large as it did in the Stone Age. The capital which might be devoted to releasing men and women, at least to some moderate degree, from the exigencies of labour is dedicated instead to the task of amassing more capital.

If the meaning-of-life question seems pressing in this situation, it is for one thing because this whole process of accumulation is ultimately as pointless and purposeless as the Schopenhaurian Will. Like the Will, capital has a momentum of its own, exists primarily for its own sake, and uses individuals as instruments of its own blind evolution. It also has something of the low cunning of the Will, persuading the men and women it employs as so many tools that they are precious, unique, and self-determining. If Schopenhauer names this deception 'consciousness', Marx calls it ideology.

Freud set out by believing that the meaning of life was desire, or the ruses of the unconscious in our waking lives, and came to believe that the meaning of life was death. But this claim can have several different meanings. For Freud himself, it means that we are all ultimately in thrall to *Thanatos*, or the death drive. But it can also mean that a life which contains nothing for which one is prepared to die is unlikely to be very fruitful. Or it can suggest that to live in an awareness of our mortality is to live with realism, irony, truthfulness, and a chastening sense of our finitude and fragility. In this respect at least, to keep faith with what is most animal about us is to live authentically. We would be less inclined to launch hubristic projects which bring ourselves and others to grief. An unconscious trust in our own immortality lies at the source of much of our destructiveness.

10. The Grim Reaper: a still from Monty Python's 'The Meaning of Life'

Wryly alert to the perishability of things, we would be wary of clutching them neurotically to our bosoms. Through this enabling detachment, we would be better able to see things for what they are, as well as to relish them more fully. In this sense, death enhances and intensifies life, rather than voiding it of value. This is not some *carpe diem* recipe, but the exact reverse. The frantic *jouissance* of seizing the day, gathering rosebuds, downing an extra glass, and living like there's no tomorrow is a desperate strategy for outwitting death, one which seeks pointlessly to cheat it rather than to make something of it. In its frenzied hedonism, it pays homage to the death it tries to disavow. For all its bravura, it is a pessimistic view, whereas the acceptance of death is a realistic one.

Besides, to be conscious of our limits, which death throws into unforgiving relief, is also to be conscious of the way we are dependent on and constrained by others. When St Paul comments that we die every moment, part of what he has in mind is perhaps the fact that we can only live well by buckling the self to the needs of others, in a kind of little death, or *petit mort*. In doing so, we rehearse and prefigure that final self-abnegation which is death. In this way, death in the sense of a ceaseless dying to self is the source of the good life. If this sounds unpleasantly slavish and self-denying, it is only because we forget that if others do this as well, the result is a form of reciprocal service which provides the context for each self to flourish. The traditional name for this reciprocity is love.

Yet we also die every minute in a rather more literal sense. We live by a kind of perpetual negation, as we annul one situation in projecting ourselves into another. This constant self-transcendence, one possible only to the linguistic animal, is known as history. Psychoanalytically speaking, however, it has the name of desire, which is one reason why desire is a plausible candidate for the meaning of life. Desire wells up where something is missing. It is a question of lack, hollowing out the

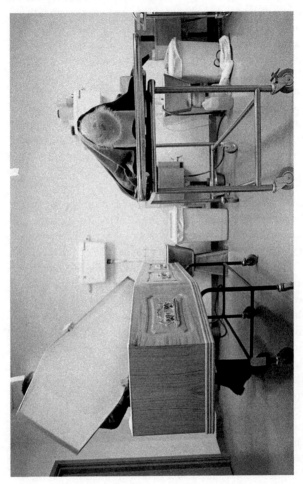

11. **From here to eternity**

present in order to shuttle us on to some similarly scooped-out future. In one sense, death and desire are antagonists, since if we ceased to desire, history would grind to a halt. In another sense, however, desire, which for Freudians is the driving force of life, reflects in its inner lack the death to which it will finally bring us. In this sense, too, life is an anticipation of death. It is only because we carry death in our bones that we are able to keep on living.

If death sounds rather too gloomy an answer to the meaning of life, and desire a rather too steamy one, what about intellectual contemplation? From Plato and Spinoza to the neo-conservative guru Leo Strauss, the idea that reflecting on the truth of existence is the noblest goal of humanity has had its allures – not least, needless to say, among intellectuals. It is pleasant to feel that one has tuned in to the meaning of the universe simply by turning into one's university office every morning. It is as though tailors, when asked about the meaning of life, should reply 'A really fantastic pair of trousers', while farmers should propose a bumper harvest. Even Aristotle, for all his interest in practical forms of life, thought this the highest form of fulfilment. Yet the idea that the meaning of life consists in pondering the meaning of life seems curiously tail-chasing. It also assumes that the meaning of life is some kind of proposition, such as 'The ego is an illusion' or 'Everything is made out of semolina'. A small elite of the wise, having devoted their lives to brooding on these matters, may then be fortunate enough to stumble on whatever the truth of the question may be. This is not exactly the case for Aristotle, for whom such speculation, or *theōria*, is itself a kind of practice; but it is a danger that the case in general can court.

Yet if life does have a meaning, it is surely not of this contemplative kind. The meaning of life is less a proposition than a practice. It is not an esoteric truth, but a certain *form* of life. As such, it can only really be known in the living. Perhaps this is what Wittgenstein had in mind when he observed in the *Tractatus* that 'We feel that even if all possible scientific questions be answered, then problems of life have still not been touched at all. Of course there is then no question left, and just this is the answer. The solution of the problem of life is seen in the vanishing of this problem' (6.52, 6.251).

What sense can we make of these cryptic sayings? What Wittgenstein probably means is not that the meaning of life is a pseudo-question, but that it is a pseudo-question as far as philosophy is concerned. And Wittgenstein had no great respect for philosophy, which he hoped his *Tractatus* would bring to an end. All the vital questions, he thought, lay outside the subject's stringent limits. The meaning of life was not something that could be said, in the form of a factual proposition; and for the early Wittgenstein, only this kind of proposition made sense. We come to glimpse something of the meaning of life when we realize that it is not the kind of thing that could be an answer to a philosophically meaningful question. It is not a 'solution' at all. Once we have recognized that it is beyond all such questions, we understand that *this* is our answer.

The words of Wittgenstein which I quoted earlier in the book – 'Not how the world is, is the mystical, but *that* it is' – mean, perhaps, that we can speak of this or that state of affairs in the world, but not of the value or meaning of the world as a whole. This does not mean that Wittgenstein dismissed such talk as nonsense, as the logical positivists did. On the contrary, he thought it far more important than talk about factual states of affairs. It was just that language could not represent the world as a whole. But though the value and meaning of the world as a whole could not be stated, they could nevertheless be shown. And one negative way of showing them was to show what philosophy could *not* say.

The meaning of life is not a solution to a problem, but a matter of living in a certain way. It is not metaphysical, but ethical. It is not something separate from life, but what makes it worth living – which is to say, a certain quality, depth, abundance, and intensity of life. In this sense, the meaning of life is life itself, seen in a certain way. Meaning-of-life merchants generally feel let down by such a claim, since it does not seem mysterious and majestic enough. It seems both too banal and too exoteric. It is only slightly more edifying than '42'. Or indeed, than the T-shirt slogan which reads 'What If The Hokey-Cokey Really Is What It's All About?' It takes the meaning-of-life question out of the hands of a coterie of adepts or *cognoscenti* and returns it to the routine business of everyday existence. It is just this kind of bathos that Matthew sets up in his gospel, where he presents the Son of Man returning in glory surrounded by angels for the Last Judgement. Despite this off-the-peg cosmic imagery, salvation turns out to be an embarrassingly prosaic affair – a matter of feeding the hungry, giving drink to the thirsty, welcoming the stranger, and visiting the imprisoned. It has no 'religious' glamour or aura whatsoever. Anybody can do it. The key to the universe turns out to be not some shattering revelation, but something which a lot of decent people do anyway, with scarcely a thought. Eternity lies not in a grain of sand but in a glass of water. The cosmos revolves on comforting the sick. When you act in this way, you are sharing in the love which built the stars. To live in this way is not just to have life, but to have it in abundance.

This kind of activity is known as *agapē*, or love, and has nothing to do with erotic or even affectionate feelings. The command to love is purely impersonal: the prototype of it is loving strangers, not those you desire or admire. It is a practice or way of life, not a state of mind. It has no connection with warm glows or personal intimacies. Is love, then, the meaning of life? It has certainly been the favourite candidate of a number of astute observers, not least of artists. Love resembles happiness in that it seems to be a baseline term, an end in itself. Like happiness, it seems to be of our nature. It is hard to say why you should bother giving water to the thirsty, not least if you know that they will die anyway in a few minutes' time.

95

In other ways, however, there are clashes between the two values. Someone who spends their life caring for a severely disabled child sacrifices their happiness to their love, even if this sacrifice is also made in the name of happiness (that of the child). Fighting for justice, which is a form of love, may bring you to your death. Love is a taxing, dispiriting affair, shot through with struggle and frustration, far removed from some beaming, bovine contentment. Yet it is still possible to argue that in the end love and happiness come down to different descriptions of the same way of life. One reason for this is that happiness is not in fact some beaming, bovine contentment, but (for Aristotle, at least) the condition of well-being which springs from the free flourishing of one's powers and capacities. And love, it can be claimed, is the same condition viewed in relational terms – the state in which the flourishing of one individual comes about through the flourishing of others.

How are we to understand this definition of love, remote as it is from both Catullus and Catherine Cookson? To begin with, we can return to our earlier suggestion that the possibility of human life having a built-in meaning does not depend on a belief in some transcendent power. It may well be that the evolution of human beings was random and accidental, but it does not necessarily follow from this that they do not have a specific kind of nature. And the good life for them may consist in realizing that nature. Bees evolved randomly as well, but can certainly be said to have a determinate nature. Bees do bee-like things. This is much less obvious in the case of human beings, since unlike bees it belongs to our nature to be cultural animals, and cultural animals are highly indeterminate creatures. Even so, it seems clear that culture does not simply annul our 'species being' or material nature. We are by nature, for example, sociable animals, who must co-operate or die; but we are also individual beings who seek our own fulfilment. To be individuated is an activity of our species being, not a condition at odds with it. We could not achieve it, for example, were it not for language, which belongs to me only because it belongs to the species first.

What we have called love is the way we can reconcile our search for individual fulfilment with the fact that we are social animals. For love means creating for another the space in which he might flourish, at the same time as he does this for you. The fulfilment of each becomes the ground for the fulfilment of the other. When we realize our natures in this way, we are at our best. This is partly because to fulfil oneself in ways which allow others to do so as well rules out murder, exploitation, torture, selfishness, and the like. In damaging others, we are in the long run damaging our own fulfilment, which depends on the freedom of others to have a hand in it. And since there can be no true reciprocity except among equals, oppression and inequality are in the long run self-thwarting as well. All this is at odds with the liberal model of society, for which it is enough if my uniquely individual flourishing is protected from interference by another's. The other is not primarily what brings me into being, but a potential threat to my being. And this, for all his celebrated belief that humans are political animals, is also true of Aristotle. He does not regard virtue or well-being as inherently relational. It is true that in his view other people are pretty essential to one's own flourishing, and that the solitary life is one fit only for gods and beasts. Yet Aristotelian man, as Alasdair MacIntyre has observed, is a stranger to love.[27]

The assumption that the meaning of life is primarily an individual affair is still alive and well. Julian Baggini writes that 'the search for meaning is essentially personal', involving 'the power and responsibility to discover and in part determine meaning for ourselves'.[28] John Cottingham speaks of a meaningful life as 'one in which the individual is engaged … in genuinely worthwhile activities that reflect his or her rational choice as an autonomous agent'.[29] None of this is false. But it reflects an individualist bias

---

[27] Alasdair MacIntyre, *A Short History of Ethics* (London, 1968), 80.

[28] Baggini, *What's It All About?*, 4, 86.

[29] Cottingham, *On the Meaning of Life*, 66.

common to the modern age. It does not see the meaning of life as a common or reciprocal project. It fails to register that there can be by definition no meaning, whether of life or anything else, which is unique to myself alone. If we emerge into being in and through one another, then this must have strong implications for the meaning-of-life question.

On the theory I have just proposed, two of the strongest contenders in the meaning-of-life stakes – love and happiness – are not ultimately at odds. If happiness is seen in Aristotelian terms as the free flourishing of our faculties, and if love is the kind of reciprocity which allows this best to happen, there is no final conflict between them. Nor is there a conflict between happiness and morality, given that a just, compassionate treatment of other people is on the grand scale of things one of the conditions for one's own thriving. There is less need, then, to worry about the kind of life which seems to be meaningful in the sense of being creative, dynamic, successful, and fulfilled, yet which consists of torturing or trampling over others. Nor, on this theory, is one forced to choose between a number of different candidates for the good life, as Julian Baggini suggests we should. Baggini proposes a range of possibilities for the meaning of life – happiness, altruism, love, achievement, losing or abnegating the self, pleasure, the greater good of the species – and suggests in his liberal fashion that there is some truth in them all. A pick-and-mix model is accordingly advanced. In designer style, each of us can take what we want from these various goods and blend them into a life uniquely appropriate for ourselves.

It is possible, however, to draw a line through Baggini's points and see most of these goods as combinable with each other. Take, as an image of the good life, a jazz group.[30] A jazz group which is improvising obviously differs from a symphony orchestra,

---

[30] I am indebted for this image to G. A. Cohen.

12. The Buena Vista Social Club

since to a large extent each member is free to express herself as she likes. But she does so with a receptive sensitivity to the self-expressive performances of the other musicians. The complex harmony they fashion comes not from playing from a collective score, but from the free musical expression of each member acting as the basis for the free expression of the others. As each player grows more musically eloquent, the others draw inspiration from this and are spurred to greater heights. There is no conflict here between freedom and the 'good of the whole', yet the image is the reverse of totalitarian. Though each performer contributes to 'the greater good of the whole', she does so not by some grim-lipped self-sacrifice but simply by expressing herself. There is self-realization, but only through a loss of self in the music as a whole. There is achievement, but it is not a question of self-aggrandizing success. Instead, the achievement – the music itself – acts as a medium of relationship among the performers. There is pleasure to be reaped from this artistry, and – since there is a free fulfilment or realization of powers – there is also happiness in the sense of flourishing. Because this flourishing is reciprocal, we can even speak, remotely and analogically, of a kind of love. One could do worse, surely, than propose such a situation as the meaning of life – both in the sense that it is what makes life meaningful, and – more controversially – in the sense that when we act in this way, we realize our natures at their finest.

Is jazz, then, the meaning of life? Not exactly. The goal would be to construct this kind of community on a wider scale, which is a problem of politics. It is, to be sure, a utopian aspiration, but it is none the worse for that. The point of such aspirations is to indicate a direction, however lamentably we are bound to fall short of the goal. What we need is a form of life which is completely pointless, just as the jazz performance is pointless. Rather than serve some utilitarian purpose or earnest metaphysical end, it is a delight in itself. It needs no justification beyond its own existence. In this sense, the meaning of life is interestingly close to meaninglessness. Religious believers who find this version of the meaning of life a little too laid-back for comfort should remind themselves that God, too, is his own end, ground, origin, reason, and self-delight, and that only by living this way can human beings be said to share in his life. Believers sometimes speak as though a key difference between themselves and non-believers is that for them, the meaning and purpose of life lie outside it. But this is not quite true even for believers. For classical theology, God transcends the world, but figures as a depth within it. As Wittgenstein remarks somewhere: if there is such a thing as eternal life, it must be here and now. It is the present moment which is an image of eternity, not an infinite succession of such moments.

Have we, then, wrapped up the question once and for all? It is a feature of modernity that scarcely any important question is ever wrapped up. Modernity, as I argued earlier, is the epoch in which we come to recognize that we are unable to agree even on the most vital, fundamental of issues. No doubt our continuing wrangles over the meaning of life will prove to be fertile and productive. But in a world where we live in overwhelming danger, our failure to find common meanings is as alarming as it is invigorating.

Further reading

1. Aristotle and virtue ethics

The text of Aristotle most relevant to this book is the *Nicomachean Ethics*, available in Penguin Classics in an edition by Jonathan Barnes (Harmondsworth, 1976). Jonathan Barnes has also published a useful introduction to Aristotle in the Very Short Introduction series (Oxford, 2000), though not much of it deals with his ethical thought. See also D. S. Hutchinson, *The Virtues of Aristotle* (London, 1986), and Jonathan Lear, *Aristotle: The Desire to Understand* (Cambridge, 1988).

More general studies of ethics relevant to the book's argument can be found in Alasdair MacIntyre, *A Short History of Ethics* (London, 1968) and *After Virtue* (London, 1981). A more recent, illuminating study is Rosalind Hursthouse, *On Virtue Ethics* (Oxford, 1999).

2. Schopenhauer

Schopenhauer's major work, and the only one referred to in this study, is *The World as Will and Representation*, ed. E. F. J. Payne, 2 vols. (New York, 1969). Useful introductions to Schopenhauer are to be found in Patrick Gardiner, *Schopenhauer* (Harmondsworth, 1963), and Brian Magee, *The Philosophy of Schopenhauer* (Oxford, 1983). A briefer account is to be found in Terry Eagleton, *The Ideology of the Aesthetic* (Oxford, 1990), ch. 7.

3. Nietzsche

Works by Nietzsche cited in this study are *The Will to Power* (New York, 1975), *Beyond Good and Evil*, and *The Birth of Tragedy*. The latter two works can be found in Walter Kaufmann (ed.), *Basic Writings of Nietzsche* (New York, 1968), a convenient selection of Nietzsche's texts. Classic introductions to his thought are Walter Kaufmann, *Nietzsche: Philosopher, Psychologist, and Antichrist* (New York, 1950); R. J. Hollingdale, *Nietzsche: The Man and his Philosophy* (London, 1964); and Arthur C. Danto, *Nietzsche as Philosopher* (New York, 1965). See also Keith Ansell Pearson, *Nietzsche* (London, 2005), and Michael Tanner, *Nietzsche* (Oxford). A more substantial study is Richard Schacht, *Nietzsche* (London, 1983).

4. Wittgenstein

The *Tractatus Logico-Philosophicus*, first published in London in 1961, is available in abridged form in Anthony Kenny (ed.), *The Wittgenstein Reader* (Oxford, 1994). See also Wittgenstein's *Philosophical Investigations*, trans. G. E. M. Anscombe (Oxford, 1953), and *Culture and Value*, trans. Peter Winch (Chicago, 1980).

For introductions to Wittgenstein's thought, see D. F. Pears, *Wittgenstein* (London, 1971), and Anthony Kenny, *Wittgenstein* (Harmondsworth, 1973). Two more recent introductions, both lucid and helpful, are A. C. Grayling, *Wittgenstein* (Oxford, 1988), and Ray Monk, *Wittgenstein* (London, 2005). Monk is also the author of an excellent biography, *Ludwig Wittgenstein: The Duty of Genius* (London, 1990). A more advanced but equally rewarding study is G. P. Baker and P. M. S. Hacker, *Wittgenstein: Understanding and Meaning* (Oxford, 1980).

5. Modernism and postmodernism

There are various allusions throughout the book to these cultural movements, which the reader might like to have further elucidated. For modernism, Peter Conrad's monumental *Modern Times, Modern*

Places (London, 1998) is worth dipping in and out of. An excellent theoretical study is Marshall Berman, *All that is Solid Melts into Air* (London, 1982). See also Raymond Williams, *The Politics of Modernism* (London, 1989), and T. J. Clark, *Farewell to an Idea* (New Haven and London, 1999).

For postmodernism, see Jean-François Lyotard, *The Postmodern Condition* (Minneapolis, 1984); Ihab Hassan, *The Postmodern Turn* (Ithaca, NY, 1987); David Harvey, *The Condition of Postmodernity* (Oxford, 1990); and Perry Anderson, *The Origins of Postmodernity* (London, 1998). Briefer studies of the trend are to be found in Alex Callinicos, *Against Postmodernism*, and Terry Eagleton, *The Illusions of Postmodernism* (Oxford, 1996). A more difficult and substantial study is Fredric Jameson, *Postmodernism, or, the Cultural Logic of Late Capitalism* (Durham, NC, 1991).

6. Marx

Marx's views on 'species being' and human nature are to be found mainly in his *Economic and Philosophical Manuscripts* of 1844. This is reprinted among other places in L. Colletti (ed.), *Karl Marx: Early Writings* (Harmondsworth, 1975). For commentaries on these matters, see Norman Geras, *Marx and Human Nature* (London, 1983), and Terry Eagleton, *The Ideology of the Aesthetic* (Oxford, 1990), ch. 8. The essay by Louis Althusser most relevant to my argument is 'On Ideology and Ideological State Apparatuses', in *Lenin and Philosophy* (London, 1971).

7. Freud

Freud's *Introductory Lectures on Psychoanalysis* (Harmondsworth, 1973) is one of the best introductions to some of his general concepts. His discussion of the death drive is to be found among other places in *Beyond the Pleasure Principle*, trans. J. Strachey, International Psycho-Analytical Library, ed. E. Jones, 4 (London, 1950). The theme is developed by Norman O. Brown in *Life Against Death* (London,

1959). For more general accounts of Freud, see Philip Rieff, *Freud: The Mind of the Moralist* (Chicago and London, 1959), and Paul Ricoeur, *Freud and Philosophy* (New Haven and London, 1970).

8. Other works

The following works are also referred to in the book:

Julian Baggini, *What's It All About?* (London, 2004).

Isaiah Berlin, *Four Essays on Liberty* (Oxford, 1969).

John Cottingham, *On the Meaning of Life* (London, 2003).

Terry Eagleton, *Against the Grain: Selected Essays 1975–1985* (London, 1986); *William Shakespeare* (Oxford, 1986); and *Sweet Violence: The Idea of the Tragic* (Oxford, 2003).

Frank Farrell, *Subjectivity, Realism and Postmodernism* (Cambridge, 1996).

Martin Heidegger, *Being and Time* (New York, 1962).

Alasdair MacIntyre, *Dependent Rational Animals* (London, 1998).

Jean-Paul Sartre, *Being and Nothingness* (London, 1958), and *Nausea* (Harmondsworth, 1963).

Roger Scruton, *Modern Philosophy* (London, 1994).

Max Weber, *Essays in Sociology*, ed. H. H. Gerth and C. Wright Mills (London, 1991).

Index

ARISTOTLE
A Very Short Introduction
Jonathan Barnes

The influence of Aristotle, the prince of philosophers, on the intellectual history of the West is second to none. In this book Jonathan Barnes examines Aristotle's scientific research, his discoveries in logic, his metaphysical theories, his work in psychology, ethics, and politics, and his ideas about art and poetry, placing his teachings in their historical context.

> 'With compressed verve, Jonathan Barnes displays the extraordinary Versatility of Aristotle, the great systematising empiricist.'
>
> **Sunday Times**

www.oup.co.uk/isbn/0-19-285408-9

MARX
A Very Short Introduction
Peter Singer

Peter Singer has succeeded in identifying the central
vision that unifies Marx's thought. He thus makes it
possible, in remarkably few pages, for us to grasp Marx's
views as a whole, rather than as an economist or a social
scientist. He explains alienation, historical materialism, the
economic theory of Capital and Marx's ideas of
communism in plain English, and concludes with an
assessment of Marx's legacy.

> 'An admirably balanced portrait of the man and his
> achievement.'

Philip Toynbee, *Observer*

www.oup.co.uk/isbn/0-19-285405-4

NIETZSCHE
A Very Short Introduction
Michael Tanner

The philosophy Friedrich Nietzsche was almost wholly
neglected during his sane life, which came to an abrupt
end in 1889. Since then he has been appropriated as an
icon by an astonishingly diverse spectrum of people,
whose interpretations of his thought range from the highly
irrational to the firmly analytical.

Idiosyncratic and aphoristic, Nietzsche is always bracing
and provocative, and temptingly easy to dip into. Michael
Tanner's readable introduction to the philosopher's life and
work examines the numerous ambiguities inherent in his
writings. It also explodes the many misconceptions
fostered in the hundred years since Nietzsche wrote,
prophetically: 'Do not, above all, confound me with what I
am not!'

'highly readable, an excellent introduction'

Guardian

www.oup.co.uk/isbn/0-19-285414-3